Challenges of Tobacco Control in the Balkans

The Case of Croatia, Bulgaria, Romania, and Greece

By

Patricia Loubeau

ISBN: 1468054066
ISBN 13: 9781468054064

Dedication

To Jean-Michel and Christian

Table of Contents

Acknowledgments

I am particularly indebted to my students in both the USA and in Eastern Europe for providing valuable research assistance and general good humour as I tried to understand their countries social and economic issues. With unfailing attention to detail, they researched and verified cigarette and commodity prices in kiosks, mini-markets and grocery stores throughout Eastern Europe. My debt of gratitude in particular is for Anastasia Chernavaska (Russia), Victor Lisnic (Moldova) and Ana Comsa (Romania).

Reference librarians on both continents were particularly helpful. A special thank you to Gergana Georgieva at the American University in Bulgaria who made multiple contacts with the Office of the Ministry of Health to verify information. Adrienne Franco, Reference Librarian at Iona College carefully helped me check each reference in the chapter on Romania and provided general reference assistance for difficult taxation issues. A special gratitude goes to the Fulbright Foundation for providing a fellowship in Croatia.

A group of my colleagues in the USA and in Eastern Europe were kind enough to review this book to insure that the analysis was robust and appropriately critical. I am indebted to these reviewers who read and re-read drafts and provided invaluable comments, criticisms and suggestions. I am especially grateful to Dr. George Priovolos, Dr. Mary Helen McSweeney-Feld, Professor Filitsa Mullen, and Professor Linda Cupit. Dr. Donald Brady was especially vigilant and thorough in his review and added numerous enhancements to the book.

In order to insure accuracy and offer an unbiased view, copies of this book were sent to the Office of the Minister of Health in each of the featured countries in this book. Comments, suggestions and verification of data were requested. Thank you to Bojan Vidović, LL.B Acting Head of State Sanitary Inspection Ministry of Health and Social Welfare Directorate for Sanitary Inspection in Croatia and Darko Milinović, MD Vice President and Minister of Health and Social Welfare for their cooperation. A special thank you to Dr. Valerija Stamenić Head of Department for Projects and Programs Directorate of Medical Affairs Ministry of Health and Social Welfare of Croatia for his review and comments.

Although legislation and public health responses are evolving, considerable effort was made to ensure the accuracy of the information contained in this book. The findings, interpretations, and conclusions expressed in this book are entirely those of the author.

Introduction

In the 1940's, my Dad was a smoker. At that time, nobody suggested that smoking was harmful. Smoking was acceptable and most adults considered it the norm. Much has changed in the last seventy years. It is now universally accepted that smoking is deleterious to health. In 2011, the tobacco epidemic will kill nearly six million people worldwide. More than five million of them will be users and ex-users of smoked and smokeless tobacco and more than 600,000 will be nonsmokers who were exposed to tobacco smoke (1). According to information available from the World Bank, for EU countries smoking is proved to be a major cause of lung cancer and other diseases (2). It is one of the largest public health problems and a cause of major concern not only among rich countries of the world but also Balkan member countries such as Greece, Bulgaria, Romania, and Croatia. The Balkan countries over the past years have been suffering from a smoking epidemic with dramatic consequences on the economy and the cost of health services. In order to reduce the incidence of smoking, most countries in the Balkans have over the past five years introduced or strengthened tobacco control measures. Some of these measures have been introduced as a result of EU mandates and others have been singularly public health measures. The overall results have been mixed. There have been some significant successes and some failures

The tobacco challenges in the Balkans are different from other areas of Europe and the rest of the world. Unlike the United States, the countries in this book have not had the benefit of standardized data collection methods, substantial government and private funding for research and education, academic support and massive social marketing efforts. Many social, economic, political and cultural factors have played a role in restricting progress in tobacco control in Croatia, Romania, Bulgaria and Greece. South East Europe (SEE) is Europe's poorest region. The cultural environment in the Balkans makes smoking normative and smoking is part of the social fabric and custom of these countries. Smuggling plays a special role in the economy of these countries. Cigarettes are commonly smuggled and the production of tobacco is part of their developing economies.

The challenges of tobacco consumption control in four countries in a specific part of Eastern Europe- namely Croatia, Bulgaria, Romania and Greece are discussed in this book. Evaluating the experience in these countries, this work meets a need for critical analysis of smoking control efforts in transitional economies and outlines a roadmap for future development. These specific countries were chosen because the author has direct experience living, working and traveling in these countries and they represent unique challenges for tobacco control. It is clear that there is a need for country-specific analytic work to provide a basis for policy making. Specifically, this book highlights data on tobacco consumption, smoking prevalence and the disease burden from tobacco use. Issues on the economics of tobacco, the tobacco industry and the policy responses developed to date to control the tobacco epidemic in southeast Europe are reviewed. Methods used included collecting data from the international PubMed database, from the World Health Organization, the European Union and the World Bank. Tobacco legislation was checked with counterparts in the studied countries and the Ministry of Health in each country were offered an opportunity to comment. Local surveys were conducted in each country to assess cigarette prices and the price of various local goods and services. Interviews were conducted with public health professionals and academics that focus on economic issues.

The tobacco industry has thwarted and impeded many tobacco control interventions. The book focuses on issues of taxation, indirect advertising by tobacco companies, high unemployment, and smuggling in countries who are attempting to meet European Union (EU) requirements for tobacco control legislation that reduces smoking consumption. These issues have until recently received little global attention. The purpose of this book is intended primarily to fill the analytic gap in understanding these problems.

The WHO Framework Convention on Tobacco Control is an international act that was negotiated under the auspices of the World Health Organization. It is one of the most successful United Nations treaties dedicated to protecting the health of the public through decreasing tobacco consumption. In order to better protect human health, parties to the treaty agree to implement certain multisectoral national tobacco control strategies. Bulgaria ratified the act in 2005, Greece and Romania ratified the act in 2006, and Croatia ratified the act in 2008. Measures, procedures and guidelines recommended by this act set the groundwork for much of the discussion in this book.

The issue of tobacco control is never a simple one and in the Balkans it is especially complex. As a result, the special circumstances that exist in this region and governmental responses or lack of response are highlighted. This information can be used to underpin the development of stronger national and regional tobacco control policies. Finally, conclusions on overall progress, challenges and opportunities are presented. It is hoped that this book will stimulate these countries to place tobacco control in its rightful place on the nation's development agenda.

References

1. WHO Report on the Global Tobacco Epidemic, 2011. World Health Organization. Available from http://whqlibdoc.who.int/publications/2011/9789240687813_eng.pdf.

2. Regional report: Europe (EU) Economics of Tobacco for Europe (EU) Region June 24, 2001. World Bank. Accessed at http://ww1.worldbank.org/tobacco/pdf.

Background

Tobacco control legislation has gained prominence at the European Union level and the rest of the world due to the serious medical effects of smoking. Smoking harms nearly every organ of the body, causing many diseases, and reduces quality of life and life expectancy. The highest recorded level of smoking was among men and was first recorded in 1948 when surveys started. At that time, 82% of men were smoking (1). It has been estimated that between 1950 and 2000, 60 million people worldwide have died from tobacco-related diseases (2). It is further estimated that by 2030 the worldwide death toll due to smoking will be around ten million annually (3).

The concern about smoking has been heightened as evidence mounts about the cost of smoking and the effects of second-hand smoke. The cost of smoking includes not only the cost of cigarettes but also medical costs, societal costs, insurance costs, and psychological costs. Smoking remains the biggest cause of avoidable death in Europe. (4)

A "smoke-free Europe" is one of the priorities of the European Commission's public health, environment, employment and research policy. Substantial steps have already been taken to promote a smoke-free environment in the EU. Progress has been achieved due to legislative efforts and diligent health promotion efforts. National legislation in the EU Member States' requires certain advertising restrictions and cigarette package labeling requirements. Some smoking control efforts (such as pictorial warnings) are optional. There are substantial differences between Member States' laws, regulations and administrative provisions on the manufacture, presentation, and sale of tobacco products.   In the early nineties, a number of enacted EU health and safety at work directives defined certain restrictions on smoking at work. These directives were complemented by the Recommendation on Smoking Prevention of 2002 which called on Member States to provide protection from exposure to environmental tobacco in in-door workplaces, enclosed public places, and public transport (5).

Italy, Malta, Sweden and parts of the United Kingdom have been cited as having excellent examples of effective measures to protect their citizens from the harmful effects of smoking. Other countries are less stringent in their legislation to restrict tobacco use. However, there is a clear trend towards smoke-free environ-ments throughout the EU Member States driven by legal require-ments and public support at the EU level. For example, many Member States have regulations banning or restricting smoking in major public places, such as health care, educational and gov-ernment facilities, and public transport.

The Balkans is a geopolitical and cultural region of southeast-ern Europe and generally refers to the countries located on or near the Balkan Peninsula. The term is used here to represent a geographical region and has no other connotations in this text. The area is situated at a major crossroads between mainland Europe and the Near East and as such has a distinct identity. The Balkan countries for the most part existed under socio-commu-nistic rule until the late 1980's and early 1990s and are now expe-riencing westernization and a move toward market economies. They suffer from a negative trade balance, a developing or poor infrastructure, and a desire to align themselves more strongly with Brussels.

Countries in this region were chosen as the topic for this book as they generally suffer from high rates of tobacco consumption and also present unique challenges in controlling this serious public health problem. The economic status of these countries is generally less than the rest of Western Europe and low- and middle-income countries increasingly bear the burden of tobacco use.

A comprehensive tobacco control strategy includes taxation, smoke-free public places, and health promotion. Reduction of smuggling is also an integral part of controlling smoking prevalence. This book deals primarily with these tobacco control issues among others in four Balkan countries, notably Croatia, Romania, Bulgaria, and Greece.

Map of the Balkans

References

1. Wald N, Nicolaides-Bouman A. UK Smoking Statistics. Oxford (UK): 2nd ed. Oxford University Press; 1991.

2. Peto R, Lopez AD, Boreham J, Thun M, Heath C Jr. Mortality from to-bacco in developed countries: indirect estimation from national vital statistics. Lancet 1992; 339:1268-1278.

3. Saffer H, Chaloupka F. The effect of tobacco advertising bans on to-bacco consumption. Journal of Health Economics.2000;19:1117-1137.

4. European Commission [homepage on the Internet] Brussels: Attitudes of Europeans towards tobacco. Special Eurobarometer 2391 waves 64.1-64.3- TNS Opinion & Social. cited 2008 Sept 20]. Available from: http://ec.europe.eu/public_opinion/archives/ebs/ebs.

5. Towards a Europe free from tobacco smoke: Policy options at EU level. [Monograph on the Internet]. Brussels: Commission of the European Communities; 2007 [cited 2007 Feb 24]. Available from; http://www.coppt.pt/docs/livro_verde.pdf.

Croatia

s a number of new nations emerged in the early nineties following the break up of the former Yugoslavia there has been a spurt of regulatory initiatives. These occurred as the new countries have moved toward nation building and inclusion into the European Union. In order to become part of the EU, a country is legally obligated to comply with and implement certain legal acts. Tobacco control legislation at the EU level consists of legally binding directives and nonbinding resolutions and recommendations regarding tobacco control (1). Croatia is currently a candidate nation for inclusion in the EU since starting accession negotiations on October 4, 2005. The government, headed by Prime Minister Zoran Milanović has made membership for Croatia in the EU a priority.

The Croatian government signed an EU accession treaty in 2011 and hopes to be admitted to the EU in July 2013. Therefore, the Croatian regulatory framework has been enacted somewhat exogenously by the process of joining the EU. Efforts to reduce tobacco consumption are not straightforward in a new country such as Croatia with both an evolving economy and a change in the political system. In this chapter the pros and cons of tobacco taxation and other tobacco control issues in the transitional economy of Croatia are analyzed.

Smoking prevalence in Croatia

In Croatia, tobacco has been consumed for centuries from both local and imported sources. During the last 100 years, the habit of cigarette smoking was prevalent, socially acceptable and considered a sign of adulthood. In a cross sectional study, 34.1% of Croatia's males and 26.6% of females between the ages of 18 and 65 were found to be daily smokers (2). For comparison, this corresponds to a rate of 24% for all adults who smoked in the United States in 1997 (3). Selected data from a study by the European Commission of 2005 data shows that the smoking prevalence of Croatia is 36% which is higher than the EU25 countries average of 33% (4) [Today there are 27 member countries in the EU]. A recent article by McDonald (2007) notes that about one-third of the adults in Croatia smoke, putting the country of 4.5 million people roughly on par with the heaviest-smoking EU member states (5). McDonald further notes that Croatians reportedly smoke 2,086 cigarettes per capita per year, compared to a European average of 1,673. With regard to the health consequences of smoking, it should be underscored that in 2002 an estimated 17% of all deaths in Croatia were caused by smoking and 80% of all cancers were lung cancer (6).

When discussing the health of a population, public health officials often refer to the "burden of disease" in a population. The burden of disease in a population can be defined as the gap between current health status and an ideal situation in which every individual lives into old age, free of disease and disability. The gap can be caused by premature mortality, disability, and certain risk factors such as tobacco, high cholesterol or obesity that contribute to illness. One summary measure that combines the impact of illness, disability, and mortality on population health is the disability-adjusted life year (DALY). The (DALY) is a commonly used metric that combines the burden of mortality and morbidity (non-fatal health problems) into a single number. The World Health Organization published a report in 2005 highlighting health issues in Croatia (7). The top risk factor identified for men in Croatia was tobacco with a total DALY's of 23.6%.

Data collection and health care research in Croatia has been hindered in part by the disruption of the war in the 1990's. During this period, there were undocumented population movements in the region that made accurate data collection difficult.

In Croatia, as elsewhere in the Balkans, antismoking regulations can be classified into two main groups - price-or tax-based policies and non-price measures. Price policies are tax based policies which are based on a given percentage of the base price. The non-price policies encompass a whole range of policies including geographic restrictions, tobacco advertising bans, sales limitations, packaging mandates, and health warnings about tobacco consumption. Tables 1 and 2 summarize the current non-price legislation on tobacco products currently in place in Croatia. This legislation includes regulation on advertising and distribution of tobacco products, smoke-free environments and health warnings.

On November 22, 2008 the Croatian Parliament passed legislation prohibiting smoking in public institutions such as hospitals, clinics, schools, nurseries and universities with infractions punishable with up to 1000 Kuna ($178.00). Notable exceptions in the Croatian Safety and Health Protection at the Workplace Act (CSHPW) are psychiatric wards in Croatia's hospitals. Historically, smoking bans in psychiatric units have led patients to smoking in secret. Also, many psychiatric units do not have safe outdoor space where patients can smoke. Even if such a space existed, the need to escort patients outside to smoke would be a considerable drain on staff time and resources.

The risk of secondhand (environmental) tobacco smoke (ETS) is well documented in the literature. Although the level of individual risk is lower than active smoking, adverse health outcomes from ETS have now been clearly documented. An important strategy to combat the adverse effects of environmental tobacco smoke is to mandate geographic restrictions regarding where tobacco can be consumed in the workplace. Countries at all stages of development are adopting bans or restrictions on smoking in the workplace. The impact of a workplace has the benefit of not only protecting people from the harm of ETS but also contributes to the reduction of tobacco consumption in the whole population. It also has a side benefit of increasing productivity as less time is lost from work for health related illnesses or smoking breaks. In Croatia, smoke-free legislation applies to all workplaces and in all rooms and closed areas where meetings and gatherings take place. However, organizations are permitted to allow smoking in certain workrooms as long as this does not infringe upon the rights of non- smokers. Specifically, the following are included in Part 11 Chapter 13 Section 63 of the CSHPW:

1. The employer shall take adequate measures to protect non-smokers from tobacco smoke.
2. Smoking during meetings shall be prohibited.
3. Smoking in workrooms and work space shall be prohibited except in the areas where the employer determines otherwise and where it shall post signs indicating that smoking is allowed.

The source of this legislation is the Croatia Safety and Health Protection at the Workplace Act, 1996. Violators of the law can be fined, the supervisor of the work area can be fined and any employer who does not properly mark the work area with a sign prohibiting smoking may be punished with a fine. Compliance with this legislation was assessed by analyzing businesses in Zagreb. The businesses in the city of Zagreb were chosen because eighty percent of the country's main industries are situated in the Zagreb-Sisak-Karlovak area. A random sample of 100 businesses were chosen. Thirty-eight large companies (with 200 or more employees) responded and were surveyed by written questionnaire. Relatively large firms were chosen for this study as they represent the greater number of workers in the Zagreb area and the requirement for a separate room for smoking may be a financial burden for the smaller employer. Also, according to the Croatian Safety and Health Protection at the Workplace Act of 1996, an employer who employs more than 50 workers is required to have at least one person serve as an occupational safety and health specialist. This person's responsibility is to monitor the application of occupational and safety health measures. According to the survey, 5 out of 38 (14%) respondents did not have a smoking policy in the workplace. In the 33 firms (86%) that did have a smoking policy, exceptions to the policy were allowed(employees could go outside of the building to smoke) or specific areas of the company were designated where smoking is permitted. Organizations are permitted under law to allow smoking in certain workrooms as long as the rights of nonsmokers are not infringed. This approach is not an ideal public health strategy. Smoking only in "designated areas" can create many problems, such as productivity loss, extra breaks, idle time and a continued health risk for the smoker. Follow-up with the human resource directors of the companies that did have a formal policy in place revealed that for many the regulation was "on paper only." Anecdotal comments from workers and supervisors included "people smoke behind closed doors," "You can smell the smoke when they open their office door," "everyone ignores the policy," "I would not ask my colleague not to smoke as it is not my business." Increased enforcement of designated smoking areas in the workplace, or even better, a total ban on smoking would do much to attenuate this "culture" of being reluctant to ask for protection of one's personal health

Pricing policies to reduce tobacco consumption are essentially tax based policies. This chapter focuses primarily on the complexities of using tax based policies to reduce consumption in Croatia.

Table 1— Legislation on advertising and distribution of tobacco products in Croatia

Description	Ban	Partial restriction	No restriction
Direct advertising of tobacco products			
National TV	X		
Cable TV	X		
National radio	X		
Local magazines, newspapers	X		
International magazines, newspapers			X
Billboards, outdoor walls	X		
Points of sale, kiosks	X		
Cinemas	X		
Indirect advertising of tobacco products			
Product placement-TV and films	X		
Sponsored events with tobacco brand name	X		
Non-tobacco products with tobacco brand names	X		
Non-tobacco product brand name used for tobacco	X		
Direct mail giveaways	X		
Promotional discounts	X		
Distribution of tobacco products through various outlets			
Vending machines	X		
Self-service displays		X	
Mail order or electronic sales		X	
Sale of single or unpacked cigarettes	X		
Sale of duty-free tobacco products		X	
Free samples of cigarettes	X		
Smoke-free areas			
Health care facilities	X		
Education facilities	X		
Government facilities	X		
Restaurants	X		
Pubs and bars		X	
Indoor workplaces and offices	X		
Theatres and cinemas	X		
Smoke-free public transport			
Buses	X		
Taxis	X		
Trains	X		
Domestic air transport	X		
International air transport	X		
Domestic water transport	X		
International water transport	X		

Table 2— Legislation in Croatia on health warnings, ingredients/constituents, number of cigarettes per pack and minimum age for buying tobacco

Description	Required/ Regulated	Comments
Minimum age for buying tobacco products	X	18 years.
Health warnings on tobacco products:	X	
Placing of the message	X	
Color, contrast, font size	X	
Area to cover	X	
Content	X	
Number of messages	X	
Language	X	
Health warnings in tobacco advertisements		Not applicable
Measurement of:		
Product ingredients	X	
Smoke constituents	X	
Content of:		
Nicotine	X	
Tar	X	
Additives	X	
Carbon monoxide	X	
PH	X	
Disclosure of ingredient or constituent information:		
To government	X	
On packages	X	
In advertisements		Not applicable
Minimum number of cigarettes per pack	X	20

Source: *Croatian Reporting Instrument to the European Union.*

The minimum age for purchasing cigarettes in Croatia is 18 years old. Interviews with smoking teenagers under 18 years old in Opatija Croatia indicates that purchasing cigarettes by underage teenagers is common and can be done without any identification. This is particularly true in small kiosks and less so in larger grocery stores like Billa. Consideration can be given to licensing retail sales outlets that sell tobacco products and verifying the date of birth of any purchaser appearing to be 25 years of age or younger. Repeat violations of laws restricting youth access should be subject to license suspension or revocation.

Pricing policies to control tobacco consumption

The ability of any government officials to use price to influence tobacco use depends on the price elasticity of demand between the original price and the higher tax included price. If the tax is large enough that the consumer is sensitive to the price change, the price elasticity of demand is elastic. Under these conditions the consumer will buy a less expensive substitute product (switch purchases to an alternative tobacco product for example) or reduce the amount of product purchased. If the tax is not large enough for the customer to mind the price change, the price elasticity of demand is inelastic. Under these conditions, the consumer will continue buying almost as much of the product as before. The law of demand still applies however, and consumers can be expected to buy a smaller quantity when price increases all other things being equal. The price elasticity of demand just influences how much less will be purchased. If the price elasticity of demand over a given price change is elastic the consumer will buy a lot less than if the price elasticity of demand is inelastic. This means that to significantly reduce purchases, the tax must be sufficiently large enough for the consumer to be unable or unwilling to continue purchase near the pre-tax level. In other words, the higher the tax included price relative to the original price must be perceived to be objectionable enough to cause the consumer to change purchasing behavior to be effective.

One of the most effective means of reducing tobacco consumption is by taxation. With respect to young people, tax increases are the most effective intervention to persuade people to quit or not to start smoking (8). Young people and others with low income tend to be highly sensitive to price increases. Because price is an especially powerful determinant of smoking initiation in youth, it significantly moderates long-term trends in cigarette consumption. In the US, a 10 percent increase in the price of cigarettes can lead to a 4 percent reduction in the demand for cigarettes. This reduction is the result of people smoking fewer cigarettes or quitting altogether (9). Although there is no available data on the impact of pricing policies on cigarette consumption in Croatia, experience from neighboring Hungary found that regular tobacco tax increases resulted in decreased cigarette consumption and lower prevalence figures in some population groups (10). Raising taxes on tobacco products is considered a highly effective component of a comprehensive tobacco control strategy.

On average, from 2001 to 2005 the price of tobacco products rose by an annual rate of 6.8% above inflation in the EU countries. For the same period, the average annual price variation in Croatia was 1.4% (11). Cigarette tax is composed of excise tax, ad valorem tax (levied as a percentage of price) and value added tax (transaction tax). According to data accessed on the Croatian Chamber of Economy web page (September 20, 2007), a pack of cigarettes (20 pieces) is taxed as follows:

Group A   0,76 € popular cigarettes
Group B   0,88 € standard cigarettes
Group C   1,51 € extra cigarettes.

Croatia lags behind those of other European countries in its use of a taxing strategy to combat smoking. The reasons are complicated. In general, government officials often hesitate to act decisively when adopting tobacco tax increases for fear that the economy may be harmed through a loss of jobs and income from growing, manufacturing, exporting and selling tobacco. The direct or indirect pro-smoking lobbying efforts also mitigate efforts to raise cigarette taxes. This is the case in Croatia.

The major tobacco company in Croatia is Tvornica Duhana Rovinj (TDR). TDR enjoys a dominant position as a Croatian taxation regime that has helped to create a monopoly at the expense of the other major players, BAT and Philip Morris. TDR is currently in a strong financial position with a new facility, solid local sales and control of much of its channels of distribution. TDR produces mainly domestic brands and had made Marlboro under license until 2005. Its flagship brand Ronhill is the most recognized and best-selling cigarette in Croatia. The most popular foreign brand is Marlboro. In 2011, TDR expanded its sales into the Russian regions of Krasnodar and Abkhazia with its popular Walter Wolf brand and plans are in place for a new factory in Iran in 2012.

TDR dominates the Croatian cigarette market by producing 75% of the local leaf tobacco production and exporting about 50% of that amount. Transnational tobacco companies have made unsuccessful attempts to enter the Croatian cigarette market. If Croatia is to achieve full integration into the EU, Croatia will have to accept free competition in the tobacco market. It is anticipated that BAT, Philip Morris and others will enter the Croatian market once harmonized EU legislation has been passed in the country.

The managers of tobacco companies have used clever strategies to circumvent Croatia's ban of tobacco advertising on billboards. TDR's management is adept at evading and undermining bans on advertising by changing the nature of the ad in ways that do not violate the law. For example, the following two billboard ads do not violate the law but effectively present the firms message. This could be classified as indirect advertising as the TDR logo and name is clearly visible on the advertisement. Joossens (1998) defines indirect advertising as follows: Indirect advertising for cigarettes includes those advertisements which, while not specially mentioning the tobacco product, tries to circumvent the advertising ban by using brand names, trademarks, emblems or other distinctive features of tobacco products (12). TDR, one of the largest producers and exporters of cigarettes in Croatia used the following in 2007 as indirect ads to promote cigarettes:

The English translation for "ma koliko mi šutjeli o tomo" is "A good product is a good product even though we are not allowed to talk about it."

TDR also produces a "sailing edition" of one of the local brands, Ronhill Lights. As you can see in the photo below, the design on the pack sends an alluring message that smoking, sailing and summer go together in Croatia.

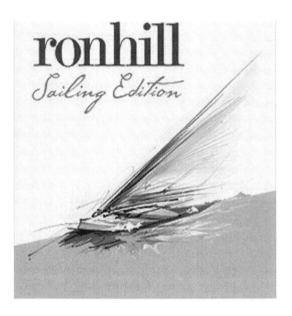

Table 3 shows the price of a pack of cigarettes* in Croatia for the most popular foreign and local brands (2011).

Table 3— Prices per pack of cigarettes* in Croatia for the most popular foreign and local brands in 2011.

Foreign brands	Price (€)	Local brands	Price (€)
Marlboro	2, 9 €	Ronhill	2, 50 €
Lucky Strike	2,68 €	Walter Wolf	2,50 €
Dunhill	3,75 €	Filter 160	2,30 €

*20 cigarettes per pack. Prices include taxes

Source: survey of prices at retailers in Zagreb Croatia.

By comparison, the price of a pack of Marlboro cigarettes in New York State is $ 10.80 (7.9 €) and in France is $ 9.22 (6.78 €). The price of a pack of Ronhill, probably the most popular domestic cigarette in Croatia is 2,50 € compared to a kilogram of apples 0,94 € (2011), one loaf of white bread 0,76 €, 10 eggs 1,07 €

(2011), a ½ liter bottle of local beer 1,68 € (2011), a concert ticket 5,76 €, a routine Veterinarian visit 10,75 € (2011). Another common measure of purchasing power parity is the cost in minutes of labor of a pack of the most popular cigarette brand. Unfortunately, no data is available for Croatia for this parameter. These prices indicate that cigarettes are relatively affordable, particularly given the availability of smuggled cigarettes which can be bought even less expensively.

The effectiveness of tax policies is undermined to the extent there are smuggled or counterfeit tobacco products on the market. Smuggled cigarettes can be sold at lower prices than legitimately produced cigarettes because taxes and duties are not paid. In fact, tobacco companies assert that increased taxation does not necessarily lead to decreased consumption and increased revenues but to increased smuggling. Recent experience in Bulgaria suggests that tax hikes while leading to a decrease in sales of cigarettes has also led to an increase in black market cigarettes. In Croatia, cigarettes are widely available on the black market. One source estimates that up to 25% of the cigarette consumption comprises smuggled cigarettes (13). Budak and colleagues (2006) report that despite increased taxes on tobacco products in Croatia since 1997, the tobacco tax revenues remain relatively unchanged (14). It is postulated that this was most likely due to an increase in black market activity.

Indeed, a carton of black market cigarettes (10 packs) can be readily purchased for 100 Kuna (approx. €13,90) from sellers standing on the street corner at Kvaternikov Trg, a major Zagreb square. A pack of Walter Wolf cigarettes smuggled from Serbia can be purchased at another prominent market on Trg Petra Kresimira in Zagreb for 10 Kuna (€1,39) per pack. Smuggled cigarettes can readily be purchased at any large fruit and vegetable market in Zagreb. Smuggling in Croatia is a complex issue. Smuggled goods are most often those that undergo transformation, or like alcohol, fuel and tobacco, are consumed. This makes the tracking of smuggled goods more difficult. Cigarettes are high import tax items which make them especially appealing for smugglers and consumers alike. Cigarette smuggling in Croatia often involves both locally produced cigarettes and major international brands such as Marlboro. Tobacco companies seem to have little incentive to reduce smuggling as lower priced cigarettes contribute to consumption. In fact, it has been suggested that smuggling is just another distribution channel for cigarette manufacturers. The common scheme for smuggling locally produced cigarettes usually involves "export" to a neighboring country, followed by illegal transport back into the country of origin. Cigarette smuggling can prosper in a region where the borders are deliberately kept porous for political reasons such as the border between Croatia and the Croat-populated Herzegovina. Smuggling is further facilitated by Croatia's ragged 5835 kilometer long coast line on the Adriatic which is difficult to patrol. Smuggling of cigarettes in Croatia can also go in the other direction. For example, cigarettes produced in Croatian tobacco factories in Zagreb and the Adriatic sea town of Rovinj were smuggled to Capljina Herzegovina and from there were transported all over Bosnia-Herzegovina as nationally produced products (15).

Corruption in countries can be a predictor and facilitator of smuggling and corruption is perceived as significant in Croatia. The government has initiated a process to overhaul areas particularly afflicted by corruption: the judicial and health systems, local governments, political party financing, public administration, and economic agencies. Citizens continue to cite corruption as one of Croatia's most important problems.

Due to the nature of import taxes and duty rates assessed on cigarette makers, smuggling can be a profitable activity. A dearth of statistics about cigarette smuggling exist because obtaining accurate information is difficult. It has been estimated that the number of smuggled cigarettes in Croatia as a percentage of domestic sales is between 25% and 49.9% (16). There are no officially published estimates for the proportion of cigarettes smuggled. To combat illicit trade, legislation needs to include measures such as requirements for package markings or creation of a system for conclusively tracking products through the entire distribution chain. A specific intra-country task force and more stringent border control may be needed to address this problem.

Map of Croatia

Croatia is not the only country with cigarette smuggling problems. The United States also suffers from cigarette smuggling. Although reliable statistics are not available, according to a spokesman for the Federal Bureau of Alcohol, Firearms, Tobacco and Explosives, in 1999 there were only 100 tobacco smuggling investigations occurred in New York state, and now there are several hundred (17). Indeed, a survey conducted in 2006 by the New York State Department of Health found that nearly half of the smokers interviewed in New York City said they had bought illegal cigarettes within the last year (18). A small sample of convenience in Croatia seems to indicate that the percentage is higher in Croatia.

Tobacco growing has a long history in Croatia dating back to the 1570's. The country brings in large profits from the tobacco industry. The main domestic product is Virginia tobacco. In 2000, the market share by cigarette manufacturer was 99% by Croatian manufacturers (19). Tobacco constitutes an important sector of agriculture and industry which contributes heavily to the national budget. In agricultural exports, Croatia has become one of the largest exporters of tobacco in the region. As smoke-free policies motivate some smokers to give up smoking, there may be a loss of profit to the tobacco industry and, consequently, reductions in tobacco-related employment. Among EU members, Croatia is particularly vulnerable in this area with a relatively high unemployment rate of 14.7 % and an average nominal monthly wage of 5018 Kuna (698€) (25).

Cigarette taxes are an important source of government revenue. TDR, one of the largest producers and exporters of cigarettes in Croatia claims that they contribute 5.5% of the total revenue of the state budget (21). The Economics of Tobacco for the Europe and Central Asia (ECA) region report confirms that cigarette tax revenue is 5 % of the total Croatian government tax revenue (22). Public health officials seem to be at cross purposes with the sector that places an emphasis on the contribution of the tobacco industry to tax revenues and values the livelihood of people who make their living from growing or selling tobacco. The majority of tobacco that is produced in Croatia is produced by small family farms (average size 4 ha) in Eastern Croatia (23) and 6,100 total hectares devoted to tobacco production (24). Family farms produce tobacco on a contract basis. About 15 % of total production comes from large producers. Four tobacco processing firms are in Croatia. Three are owned by the tobacco factory Rovinj (TDR). All of these producers contribute to the national employment rate in a country that is working hard to stimulate its economy. These factors contribute to the push/pull of health versus economy. Still, taxation remains a powerful tool, particularly in the young, to discourage smoking. Additional taxation with revenues earmarked specifically for public health efforts could be imposed.

Conclusions

Overall, Croatia does not fare badly in terms of implementing antismoking policies compared to other countries in transition. On the positive side, more Croat smokers and ex-smokers were exposed to anti-smoking campaigns than smokers in other European countries (25). The issue of tobacco control in Croatia however, is not a simple one and requires a multi-pronged approach.

Croatia has accepted and embraced the modern concept of health promotion, which intends to improve the level of public health by tackling health determinants and not just preventing disease. For example, the Andrija Stampar School of Public Health in Zagreb Croatia offers general health care education as well as seminars and programs to reduce smoking consumption. National public health interventions include self help material, "say yes to no smoking program," school based educational programs, "quit and win" contest for smoking cessation and others. Effective efforts directed toward the entire population is needed to encourage individuals to stop smoking. Ideally, action should include age- and gender-based promotional and educational programs. Treatment for smokers should be provided by the government either at reduced cost or free of charge. Training in smoking cessation should be part of the basic curriculum for all health professionals. Even brief and simple advice from health professionals can have a substantial increase in smoking cessation rates. A primary focus of all primary health care providers (nurses, physicians, dentists and pharmacists) should address education about smoking cessation when appropriate.

The regulation about smoking in public places and the workplace should become more restrictive and there is the outstanding issue of effective enforcement of existing regulations. Current regulation should be enforced with very heavy penalties and litigation if necessary. Sanitation inspectors who oversee the implementation of the regulation have recently begun to provide quarterly automatic reports to the Minister of Health on what was found and the action taken. This is a very positive step. Specifically, smoking should be banned in all public places including restaurants, pubs, bars and public transportation. Also, social marketing efforts should stress non smoker's rights to enjoy a smoke free environment so that individuals will be less tolerant of public exposure to second hand smoke.

Additional efforts are needed with respect to the advertising of tobacco. It is suggested that legislation be enacted to ban advertising at point of sale, kiosks, and in the cinema. Regarding promotion, sponsorship, and all forms of indirect advertising, the country would be wise to adopt a total ban on advertising.

It is well known that cigarettes are addictive. The Institute of Medicine, a unit of the National Academy of Sciences, has called for a gradual reduction of the nicotine content of all cigarettes to non-addictive levels (26). While this is a worthy strategy and should be considered as an amendment to Croatian law, this would take years to eliminate addiction. A firmer strategy would be one that includes raising cigarette taxes, a complete ban of smoking in public places, enforcing the laws against selling tobacco to children, and offering free or inexpensive help to smokers trying to quit. Finally, an economic package that stimulates the economy and reduces the burden of unemployment will do much to close the gap between those who feel the need for tobacco revenues and those who place a higher value on individual human life.

The economic future of the relatively new nation of Croatia has potential for improvement given the countries natural assets and human talents. In terms of income per capita, Croatia is ahead of Bulgaria and Romania. Further, Western European endorsement of its candidacy for EU membership adds strength to its economic development. Placing a high value on and preserving health is consistent with a forward moving country in the 21st century. The challenge for this young emerging country with a persistently high unemployment rate, slowing export growth, and weak credit growth is a state budget that includes a large contribution from tobacco tax revenue. However, the long term societal cost of smoking vastly outweighs any short term gains.

References

1. World Health Organization [database on the Internet] [cited 2008 Jul 30] Available from: http://www.smokefreeengland.co.uk/files/who-euro.pdf.

2. Turek S, Rudan I, Smolej-Narancic N, Szirovicza L, Cubrilo-Turek M, Zerjavic-Hrabak,V, et al. A large cross-sectional study of health attitudes, knowledge, behavior and risks in the post-war Croatian population (The First Croatian Health Project). Coll Antropol, 2001 Jun; 25(1):77-96.

3. Healthy People 2010: Understanding and Improving Health, U.S. Department of Health and Human Services, Public Health Service; 2000. [Cited 2007 Jul 9]. Available from: http://www.healthypeople.gov/default.htm.

4. European Commission [homepage on the Internet] Brussels: Attitudes of Europeans towards tobacco. Special Eurobaromcter 2391 waves 64.1-64.3- TNS Opinion & Social. Cited 2008 Sept 20]. Available from: http://ec.europe.eu/public_opinion/archives/ebs/ebs.

5. MacDonald, Neil. Zagreb's smokers wake up and smell the coffee A forward-looking cafe in Croatia's capital has defied the nation's nicotine addiction for an aromatic blend. :[USA 1ST EDITION]. Financial Times. 2007 Apr 17. In: ABI/INFORM Global [database on the Internet] [cited 2008 Sep 21]. Available from: http://www.proquest.com.rocky.iona.edu:2048/ Document ID: 1256036571.

6. Hrabak-Zerbajic V. Country report on advertising and promotion bans-Croatia [monograph on the Internet]. California: University of California; 2004 [cited 2008 Sep 18]. Available from: http://repositories.cdlib.org/tc/whotcp/Croatia2004.

7. Highlights on Health in Croatia, 2005. World Health Organization, Regional Office for Europe. [Cited 2007 Sept 15] Available from: http://www.euro.who.int/highlights.

8. Green, L W. Taxes and the tobacco wars. Canadian Medical Association Journal. 1997 Jan 15; 156 (2): 205-206. In: ProQuest Health Management [database on the Internet] [cited 2008 Sep 21]. Available from: http://www.proquest.com/;Document ID: 418440181.

9. Adapted from Achievements in Public Health, 1990-1999: Tobacco Use, Morbidity and Mortality Weekly Report; 48, (43): 986-993.The Centers for Disease Control and Prevention, 1999.

10. Szilágyi-Tibor. Higher cigarette taxes-healthier people, wealthier state: the Hungarian experience. Cent. Eur J Public Health. 2007 Sep; 15 (3):122-6.

11. The European Tobacco Control Report. World Health Organization. Regional Office for Europe; 2007 [cited 2008 Jun 9]. Available from: http://www.euro.who.int/document/e89842.

12. Joossens, Luk. (1998) Why Ban Tobacco Advertising in the European Union.Global Link. Resources on Tobacco Control

13. Eastern Europe: EU expansion offers opportunities and challenges. Source from: World Tobacco News article id: 13483; 28 January 2008. [Cited 2008 Jun 2]. Available from http://act.tobaccochina.net/english-new/content1.aspx?id=36723.

14. Budak J, Goel R.K, Nelson, M.A. Smoking prevalence and antismoking regulations in transition countries. Transition Studies Review. (2006) 13(1):231-248.

15. Hajdinjak, M. Smuggling in Southeast Europe. Center for the study of democracy. 2002 [cited 2008 Apr 15]. Available from: http://pdc.ceu.hu/archive/00001572/01/Smuggling_in_SE_EU.pdf.

16. Mackay J. Ericksen M. Tobacco Atlas. Brighton (UK): Myriad Editions; 2002.

17. Medaglia A. Cigarettes are costly, but often less so in Chinatown. New York Times.2007 Sep 18; sect.B:2 (col.0).

18. Croatia: Quarterly economic indicators. Eiu ViewsWire. New York: Aug 13, 2008 [cited 2008, Sep 20]. Available from: http://proquest.umi.com/pqdweb?index=5&did=1547206931&SrchMode=1&sid=2&Fmt=.

19. Tobacco Control Country Profiles. 12th World Conference on Tobacco Control and Health; Aug 2003. Helsinki (FI). Available from: http://www.cancer.org/downloads/TOB/Croatia.pdf.

20. New York State Department of Health, Cigarette Purchasing Patterns among New York Smokers: Implications for Health, Price, and Revenue, March 2006. Prepared by RTI International.

21. Tvornica Duhana Rovinj Corporate Website [cited Sept. 7, 2007] Available from URL: http: www.tdr.hr/eng/corporate/index.html

22. World bank. Economics of tobacco for the Europe and central Asia (ECA) Region. May 20, 2001. [Cited Sept 17, 2008] Available from: http://siteresources.worldbank.org/INTETC/.

23. Croatia Tobacco and Products Report 2001 prepared by Marija Radman USDA Foreign Agricultural Service *Gain* Report. GAIN Report # HR 1001 March 7, 2001. Available from: http://www.fas.usda.gov/gainfiles/200103/65679911.pdf.

24. USDA, Economic Research Service, Tobacco Statistics. (94102) Table 167 World Cigarette Production Selected Countries, 1960-1995, USDA Website. Available from: http://www.ers.usda.gov/

25. Goel RK, Budak J. Smoking patterns in Croatia and comparisons with European nations. Cent Eur J Public Health. 2007 Sep; 15 (3):110-5.

26. Bonnie RJ, Stratton K, Wallace RB, editors. Ending the Tobacco Problem. Washington (DC): Institute of Medicine of the National Academies; 2007.

Bulgaria

As a member of the EU, a country is legally obligated to comply with and implement certain legal acts. Tobacco control legislation at the EU level consists of legally binding directives and nonbinding resolutions and recommendations regarding tobacco control (1). Since 1946, Bulgaria was under the Soviet sphere of influence. Communist domination ended in 1990, when Bulgaria held its first multiparty election. In 1991, Bulgaria became a parliamentary democracy, and since January 2007, the country has been a member of the European Union. As such, the Bulgarian regulatory framework has also been enacted somewhat exogenously by the process of joining the EU. Efforts to reduce tobacco consumption are difficult to implement in a country with both an evolving economy, a change in the political system and a history of public bribery. Bulgaria has made some progress in developing tobacco control programs partially as a result of accession into the EU. The pros and cons of tobacco taxation in this transitional economy and other issues are examined in this chapter.

Smoking prevalence in Bulgaria

Tobacco has been grown, consumed, and exported in Bulgaria for centuries. Tobacco smoking is thought to have been introduced to the Balkan Peninsula by Italian merchants probably at the end of the nineteenth century. Tobacco production has been developed on a broad industrial base since the turn of the twentieth century. In fact, tobacco production has traditionally been one of Bulgaria's largest economic sectors. In the beginning, only oriental varieties were cultivated in Bulgaria. In accordance with world trends, the cultivation of light tobacco trends (Virginian and Burley) began to be cultivated. The traditional oriental brand, however, remains the dominant share produced.

During the last 100 years, the habit of cigarette smoking in Bulgaria was highly prevalent, socially acceptable and considered a sign of adulthood. Data available from the Bulgarian National Statistical Institute taken from the European Health Survey 2008 found that 40.5 % of males and 18.9% of females are daily smokers. The very vulnerable age group between 15 and 24 years old showed that 27.7% of males and 17.9 % of females are daily smokers (2). For comparison, an estimated 19.8 percent of U.S. adults were current smokers in 2007(3).

The prevalence of current tobacco smoking is a predictor of the future burden of tobacco-related diseases. According to World Health Statistics 2010, the prevalence of smoking any tobacco product among adults aged 15 years or older in 2006 was 49% for males and 38 % for females. This compares with 21.5% prevalence for males and 16.6% prevalence for females for the European region in general (4). A wide variation in smoking prevalence exists among EU 27 members. The proportion of people aged 15 years and over that smoke in the EU-27 ranges from a low of 16% in Sweden to a high of 38% in Greece. The most recent comparable data for Bulgaria is for 2001 and indicates that 32.7% of those aged 15 years and over smoke. (5). Bulgaria ranks second only to Greece as the European country with the highest percentage of smokers (6). According to expert estimation, smoking causes directly or indirectly some 20% of all Bulgarian deaths *(7)*.

Antismoking efforts in Bulgaria are affected in two ways – price -or tax-based policies and non-price measures. The non-price policies encompass a whole range of policies including geographic restrictions, tobacco advertising bans, sales limitations, packaging mandates, and health warnings about tobacco consumption.

Tables 1 and 2 summarize the current legislation on tobacco products currently in place in Bulgaria. These tables detail non-price measures used to restrict alcohol products.

The WHO Framework Convention on Tobacco Control (FCTC) calls for large clear health warnings on tobacco packages that 'may be in the form of words or include pictures or pictograms and cover at least 30% of the principal display areas. Well-designed package health warnings are effective at reducing tobacco consumption. In general, there has been progress in the Balkans in implementing package warnings, which is very encouraging. As noted in Table 2, tobacco warnings are required under Bulgarian law. The first cigarette pack warnings that appeared on Bulgarian cigarettes were not really a warning because the original text could be translated to read "People who do not smoke will die healthy."

33

Table 1—Legislation on advertising and distribution of tobacco products

Description	Ban	Partial restriction	No Restriction
Direct advertising of tobacco products			
National TV	X		
Cable TV	X		
National radio	X		
Local magazines, newspapers	X		
International magazines, newspapers			X
Billboards, outdoor walls	X		
Points of sale, kiosks		X	
Cinemas	X		
Indirect Advertising of tobacco products			
Product placement- TV and films	X		
Sponsored events with tobacco brand name	X		
Non-tobacco products with tobacco brand names	X		
Non-tobacco product brand name used for tobacco	X		
Direct mail giveaways	X		
Promotional discounts	X		
Distribution of tobacco products through various outlets			
Vending machines			X
Self-service displays			X
Mail order or electronic sales			X
Sale of single or unpacked cigarettes	X		
Sale of duty free tobacco products	X		
Free samples of cigarettes	X		
Smoke- free areas			
Health care facilities	X		
Education facilities	X		
Government facilities	X		
Restaurants		X	
Pubs and bars		X	
Indoor workplaces and offices	X		
Theatres and cinemas	X		
Smoke-free public transit			
Buses and taxis	X		
Trains		X	
Domestic air transport	X		
International air transport	X		

Table 2— Legislation on health warnings, ingredients/
constituents, number of cigarettes per pack and
minimum age for buying tobacco.

Description	Required/ Regulated	Not required/ regulated	No data Available	Comments
Minimum age for buying tobacco products	X			18 years
Health warnings on tobacco products:	X			Size of warning 4%
Placing of the message	X			
Color, contrast, font size	X			
Area to cover	X			
Content	X			
Number of messages	X			
Language	X			
Pictorial warnings		X		
Measurement of:				
Product ingredients	X			
Smoke constituents	X			
Content of:				
Nicotine	X			
Tar	X			
Additives		X		
Carbon monoxide		X		
PH			X	
Disclosure of ingredient or constituent information:				
To government	X			
On packages	X			
In advertisements				N/A
Minimum number of cigarettes per pack	X			20

Source: *Bulgarian Reporting Instrument to the European Union.*

Pricing policies to control tobacco consumption

In all of the Balkan nations, an effective means of reducing tobacco consumption is by taxation. With respect to young people, tax increases are the most effective intervention to persuade people to quit or not to start smoking (8). Young people and adults with low income tend to be highly sensitive to price increases. Price has an influence on whether or not young people begin to smoke, and influences long-term trends in cigarette consumption. In the Balkan region as elsewhere, raising taxes on tobacco products is considered a highly effective component of a comprehensive tobacco control strategy. This is especially true if it is coupled with effective anti-smuggling efforts.

Taxes on cigarettes are of two types-excise and VAT. An excise tax is a tax on tobacco produced for sale within a country or imported and sold in that country. It can be either specific (a set amount per pack) or ad valorem (an amount proportional to the cost of the pack).

VAT (value added tax) may be charged in addition to excise tax. The VAT imposed tends to be on a base that includes the excise tax and custom duty. According to data from the World Health Organization, the structure of taxation for tobacco products 2006 for Bulgaria for filtered cigarettes is as follows:

Specific excise	15.93%
Ad valorem excise	31.80%
VAT	16.67%
Total Tax	64.40%

In EU countries, total taxes can exceed 75% of the selling price of a pack of cigarettes when value-added tax (VAT) is included (9).

Bulgaria lags behind other Western European areas in its use of a taxing strategy to combat smoking. The reasons are allegedly economic and political. There seems to be a push/pull phenomena that exists between the goals of the ministry that is responsible for health and the ministry that concerns itself with economics and trade.

The direct or indirect pro-smoking lobbying efforts also mitigate efforts to raise cigarette taxes. This is the case in Bulgaria.

The chief tobacco company in Bulgaria was the state-owned Bulgartabac which was established by the government in 1947. It was a major regional producer of cigarettes with large export markets in Eastern Europe and the Soviet Union during communism. Bulgartabac enjoys a dominant position as a Bulgarian taxation regime that has helped to create a monopoly at the expense of the other major players. Many transnational tobacco companies have expressed an interest in the privatization of Bulgartabac. Bulgartabac is a major regional cigarette producer with large export markets in Eastern Europe. Its flagship brand Victory is the most recognized and best-selling cigarette in Bulgaria. Bulgartabac was state-owned until 2011 when VTB Capital bought the state's 79.83 per cent stake in Bulgartabac Holding for 100.1 million euro. As a state owned monopoly, Bulgartabac's inefficiencies were most likely a public health benefit. Private tobacco companies tend to market their products heavily, aggressively push to expand their chain of distribution, and are more likely to challenge public health attempts to control tobacco use.

Table 3 shows the price of a pack of cigarettes* in Bulgaria for the most popular foreign and local brands (2010).

Table 3—Prices per pack of cigarettes* in Bulgaria for the most popular foreign and local brands in 2010.

Foreign brands	Price (€)	Local brands	Price (€)
Marlboro	5.50 BGN (2, 82 €)	Victory	4, 60 BGN (2, 35 €)
Winston	4.70 BGN (2, 41 €)	G& D	4, 10 BGN (2, 10 €)
Camel	4.50 BGN (2, 30 €)	Melnik	4,00 BGN (2, 05 €)

*20 cigarettes per pack. Prices include taxes

The price of a pack of Victory, the most popular domestic cigarette in Bulgaria is 4,60 BGN compared to a kilogram of apples 1.10 BGN, one loaf of white bread 1 BGN, 10 eggs 1.70 BGN, a ½ liter bottle of local beer (Zagorka) 0,66 BGN, a movie ticket 4,0 BGN, a routine Veterinarian visit 15 BGN. As in Croatia, these prices indicate that cigarettes in Bulgaria are relatively affordable, particularly given the availability of smuggled cigarettes which can be bought on the black market even less expensively.

Smuggling

In general, the transition from totalitarian rule to democracy has been associated with the growth of crime in many countries throughout the world. Bulgaria is no exception. Corruption and organized crime are linked to cigarette smuggling and are admittedly widespread in Bulgaria. In fact, serious doubts were expressed about whether Bulgaria was ready to join the EU in 2007 because of rampant corruption.

The smuggling of goods is an important source of income for various groups ranging from Bulgarian political leaders and government officials to people living in border areas. Cigarettes represent one of the most popular items for smuggling due to their specific characteristics (small size, high price, very large consumption, lack of perishability, easy resalability, and high import tax rates). Profits made from smuggling cigarettes can be huge. The illicit trade volume of cigarettes sold in Bulgaria increased significantly over the course of 2009. According to the Euromonitor, the main reason is the growing prices of legally taxed cigarettes and the relatively low income of Bulgarian con-sumers (10). The effectiveness of tax policies is undermined to the extent there are smuggled or counterfeit tobacco products on the market. Smuggled cigarettes are significantly less expensive because taxes and duties are not paid. In fact, tobacco compa-nies assert that increased taxation does not necessarily lead to decreased consumption and increased revenues but to increased smuggling. Additionally, smuggling allows popular international brands such as Marlboro, Camel and Salem to become affordable to low income consumers and to image conscious young people in developing countries.

Tax hikes in Bulgaria have led to a decrease in sales of cigarettes but also to an increase in the sale of black market cigarettes. One source estimates that up to 15% of the cigarette consumption comprises smuggled cigarettes (11). In Bulgaria, cigarettes are widely available on the black market. A carton of black market cigarettes (10 packs) can be readily purchased for 10 BGN (approx. 5.12 €) less per carton than regularly priced cigarettes. A single pack of smuggled Victory cigarettes is 2,75BGN on the black market. Smuggling in Bulgaria is a major issue. Goods that are smuggled are most often those that tend to be changed in some way or like alcohol and tobacco, are consumed. This makes the tracking of smuggled goods more complicated. Cigarettes are high import tax items with an addictive component which make them especially appealing for smugglers and consumers alike. Cigarette smuggling in Bulgaria involves both locally produced cigarettes and major international brands such as Marlboro. In one example, cigarette boxes were loaded and were legally exported from the Black Sea port of Varna. Several miles from shore, smugglers moved the cigarettes to another ship and transported them back to Bulgaria. In an attempt to escape from authorities and hide the evidence the captain tied to sink the ship.

Tobacco companies seem to have little incentive to reduce smuggling as lower priced cigarettes contribute to consumption whether the taxes are paid or not. The common scheme for smuggling locally produced cigarettes in the Balkans usually involves "export" to a neighboring country, followed by illegal transport back into the country of origin. Cigarette smuggling can prosper in a region where the borders are kept relatively loose for political reasons such as the border between Bulgaria and Greece, Macedonia, Serbia and Romania. Visas are no longer required between Bulgaria, Macedonia and Serbia. The end of visas has led to an increase in the so-called "suitcase trade" in cigarettes between these countries(12). The "suitcase trade" involves people crossing national frontiers on foot carrying suitcases or bags. Suitcase carriers reach the nearest central market place in a neighboring country and sell their "goods." The 378 kilometer long coast line on the Black Sea which is difficult to effectively patrol is also conducive to smuggling.

Map of the Black Sea coast of Bulgaria.

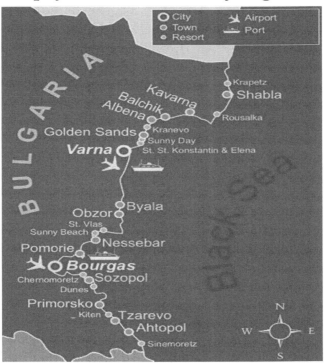

According to the Center for the Study of Democracy, duty-free trade–related smuggling of excise goods has been one of the most potent and sustainable sources of political corruption in Bulgaria for the last fifteen years(13).The operation of duty-free outlets has been a major channel for flooding the Bulgarian market with tons of illegal cigarettes. Duty free trade is concentrated in the hands of a few politically connected individuals who exert governmental and political pressure to keep them open.

Duty-free shops are tolerated despite promises to the EU to close these shops. Several attempts have been made to close them down but it is speculated that the duty-free owners have strong links to government officials and party leaders. This is despite opposition from law enforcement. In July of 2008, Bulgarian authorities closed down all the duty free shops along the country's land borders with non-EU member states. Permanent closure of these shops on all borders including airports, seaports and Bulgarian airlines would be a test of the government's commitment to fight corruption and to strengthen public health measures.

Due to high import taxes and duty rates, smuggling cigarettes can be a profitable activity especially in an area where job opportunities are limited. In addition to smuggled cigarettes the incidence of counterfeit cigarettes continues to diversify and grow in Bulgaria. A recent rash of counterfeit "Victory White" cigarettes marked "For duty free sale only" has been intercepted in a number of cities in Bulgaria. These cigarettes contained low grade tobacco and excessive levels of nicotine.

Statistics of cigarette smuggling in Bulgaria are difficult to locate as the topic does not lend itself to reliable and readily available data collection. The volume of cigarette smuggling can be most accurately determined if the data from customs statistics are compared with the data from marketing research on the sales of imported cigarettes in the country. According to the latter, the annual cigarette market in the country can be estimated at 500-560 million BGN. Imported cigarettes represent 12-15 percent of all cigarettes sold (60-80 million BGN). Based on these estimates, experts calculated that in 1999, less than 10 percent of imported cigarettes, sold in Bulgaria, were legally imported (14). The head of Bulgartabac estimated that in 2008, smuggled cigarettes in Bulgaria account for 30-40% of the market (15). There are no officially published estimates for the proportion of cigarettes smuggled.

To combat illicit trade, legislation needs to include measures such as requirements for licensing, high-tech markings, country specific tax stamps or creation of a system for conclusively tracking and monitoring products through the entire distribution chain. A specific intra-country task force between Bulgaria, Macedonia, Greece, and Romania and more stringent border control may be needed to address this problem. In addition, since tobacco smuggling rises with corruption, general government policies to stem corrupt activities in Bulgaria should be part of an overall plan to reduce tobacco consumption. This admittedly may be difficult to accomplish in a country where it is alleged that the smuggling of excise goods has been a source of funding for political parties.

Unemployment

After the collapse of the communist regime, the country experienced a long and challenging transition period in the 1990's with changes in the labor market. Under the previous socialist regime, unemployment was essentially non-existent due to pronounced job security. Everyone had a job and determination of compensation was centralized. Bulgaria's painful transition from a centrally planned economy to market-oriented capitalism has resulted in economic and social upheaval. Although small businesses and entrepreneurs emerged, the transition to a market economy has resulted in a high jobless rate, increasing inequality of incomes, and de-industrialization. Bulgarians experience some of the lowest incomes in Europe. Unemployment is a burning topic for the current center-right government, irrespective of the considerable differences in data about unemployment in various official sources. Although Bulgaria has experienced a natural decrease in tobacco production, tobacco growing has always provided employment in Bulgaria. The country brings in large profits from the tobacco industry. The main domestic product is oriental tobacco. Bulgarian farmers (who are mostly Bulgarian

Muslims) receive an EU subsidy which is determined by the size of their land. Although there is a lack of official statistics, tobacco constitutes an important sector of agriculture and industry which contributes heavily to the national budget. In agricultural exports, Bulgaria is one the largest exporters of tobacco in the region. The European Commission Directorate General Taxation and Customs Excise Duty tables note that the Bulgarian government received 1764,01 BGN (901,94 €) *(in millions)* in revenue on consumption (excise duties and similar charges) of cigarettes in 2009 (16). As smoke-free policies motivate some smokers to give up smoking, there may be a loss of profit to the tobacco industry and, consequently, reductions in tobacco-related employment. For decades, Bulgarian tobacco regions, populated mostly by Bulgarian Muslims, have produced only tobacco and nothing else, leaving the farmers with no crop alternative. Among EU members, Bulgaria feels it is particularly vulnerable in this area with a relatively high unemployment rate of 9.1 % and an average nominal monthly wage of BGN 563 (293 €) (17). The government has reported that as of 2008, the Ministry of Agriculture has developed a special program for the gradual replacement of tobacco with economically viable alternative activities (18). The Ministry has been queried for specific details about this program but as of this printing has not yet responded to a request for detailed information.

Bulgaria could conceivably derive overall net economic gains, not losses, if demand for tobacco products fell. This is because economic losses would be offset by economic gains at the household level and decreased health care costs at the national level. These household economic gains will result from more disposable income as money will not be spent on cigarettes.

Taxation

State-owned cigarette manufacturer Bulgartabac has a market share of more than 90% of the cigarettes sold legally on the market

(19). Bulgarian state revenue is significantly enhanced by the contribution of tobacco taxes which were increased in 2009 and 2010. (20). Public health officials seem to be in conflict with the sector that places an emphasis on the contribution of the tobacco industry to tax revenues and values the livelihood of people who make their living from growing or selling tobacco. Bulgaria is one of South East Europe's main tobacco leaf producers and exporters and has the largest land area for tobacco growing. Traditionally, tobacco production has been a large economic sector for Bulgaria due in part to the country's soil and climate as well as decades of state support for production. Traditionally, the Muslim population has grown tobacco in Bulgaria. The majority of tobacco leaf that is produced in Bulgaria is produced by small family (lineal) farms concentrated in the Central, Southern and South-Western part of Bulgaria (21) and 36,500 total hectares are devoted to tobacco production (22). Family farms receive state support and produce tobacco on a contract basis. There are eleven tobacco leaf processing firms and one cigarette factory in Bulgaria. Bulgartabac employs seasonal workers in addition to about 8500 permanent workers. All of these producers contribute to the national employment rate in a country that is working hard to stimulate its economy. These factors contribute to the push/pull of health versus economy. Still, taxation remains a powerful tool, particularly in the young, to discourage smoking. Additional taxation with revenues earmarked specifically for public health efforts could be imposed. Transparent governmental monitoring would need to be put in place to insure that allocated revenues were direct increases to the public health budget.

Conclusions

Progress on health reforms related to tobacco control in Bulgaria has been slow. On May 21, 2009, the Bulgarian Parliament enacted a law making restaurants, bars, clubs, and cafes 100%

smoke free. Before the new law went into effect, members of parliament delayed the full smoking ban citing economic concerns for unemployment and tourism. According to members of the hotel and restaurant sector, an extension was necessary so preparations could be made to compensate for the anticipated financial losses. The southwest town of Kyustendil is the only place in Bulgaria where a full ban on smoking in public places is enforced. On a more positive note, 1 % of tobacco and excise duties were to be used to finance national programs on tobacco alcohol and drugs from 2007 to 2010 (23). Whether these funds were used for services that would not have been otherwise provided is not known.

The health care system in Bulgaria is plagued with funding shortages, nationwide strikes by physicians, multiple changes in the health minister and a gross inequality of access. Reliable data on how this 1% allocation of tobacco excise taxes was actually spent is not readily available. The issue of tobacco control in Bulgaria is not a simple one and like elsewhere in the Balkans, requires a multi-pronged approach.

The modern concept of health promotion and disease prevention is accepted in theory in Bulgaria. Efforts aimed at the entire population are needed to encourage individuals to stop smoking. Ideally, action should include age- and gender-based (especially young and males) promotional and educational programs. Treatment for smokers who would like to quit should be free of charge. Training in smoking cessation should be part of the basic curriculum for all types of health professionals. Even brief and simple advice from health professionals can have a substantial increase in smoking cessation rates. Smoking cessation conversations are not regularly included in preventive care or acute care visits.

The regulation about smoking in public places and the workplace should become more restrictive and there is the outstanding issue of effective enforcement of existing regulations. Anecdotal information implies that the regulations tend to be ignored. Current regulation should be enforced with very heavy penalties and litigation if necessary. Sanitation inspectors who oversee the implementation of the regulation should provide periodic automatic reports to the Minister of Health on what was found and the action taken. Specifically, smoking should be effectively banned in all public places including restaurants, pubs, bars and public transportation. Admittedly this is difficult as Bulgaria is very much an outdoor "café society". Since smoking is highly prevalent among the adult population in cafes, there is a certain degree of solidarity between them to ignore any pressure to refrain from smoking. Social marketing efforts should stress non smokers' rights to enjoy a smoke free environment. People should be exulted to respect the rights of others that do not want to be exposed to second hand smoke.

Additional efforts are needed with respect to the advertising of tobacco. In 2011, a popular cigarette company engaged young women in bright alluring costumes to pass out free cigarettes to the students of both the American University in Bulgaria and Southwest University in Blagoevgrad Bulgaria. Legislation should be enacted to ban advertising at point of sale, kiosks, and on billboards. Regarding promotion, sponsorship, sales promotions and all forms of indirect advertising, the country would be wise to adopt a total ban on advertising.

In Bulgaria, Smoking hazards are printed in direct health warning labels on cigarette boxes. One side of the box says "Пушачите умират по-млади" (Smokers die younger) and the other side says "Пушенето вреди сериозно на Вас и на другите около Вас" (Smoking hurts you and the people around you). Since 2004, it has been possible to accompany written warning labels with a picture. However, to date no cigarette producers have opted to include pictures. Pictorial health warnings on the two main sides of tobacco products would serve to strengthen the health warning. Evidence from countries where pictorial warnings have already been introduced indicates that images have a greater impact than text warnings alone (24). Rotating these pictures on a regular basis would enhance the health promotion message.

A gradual reduction of the nicotine content of all cigarettes to non-addictive levels is a worthy strategy and should be considered as an amendment to Bulgarian law for this highly resistant population. A progressive strategy for Bulgaria would be one that includes raising cigarette taxes, a complete ban of smoking in public places, enforcing the laws against selling tobacco to children, and offering free or inexpensive counseling and pharmacotherapy to smokers trying to quit. Finally, an economic package that stimulates the economy and reduces the burden of unemployment will help to close the gap between those who feel the need for tobacco revenues and those who place a higher value on individual human life. Recently, Bulgaria has taken much needed steps to facilitate business development. The country has expanded the highway infrastructure, attracted new industrialization such as Russian and Chinese vehicle manufacturers and the food giant Unilever and begun to look at solar power ventures. Further business development outside of the tobacco interests will decrease the reliance on this industry and reduce the need for tobacco tax revenues.

The country of Bulgaria has many natural assets and talented and committed professionals. The Bulgarian people, however, do not seem to expect much from their politicians and bureaucrats. The country seems to have suffered from being under the thumb of a "pause" button in many areas of development under communism. Placing a high value on and preserving the health of its citizens is consonant with a forward moving EU member. Although this is a challenge for a young democratic government with high unemployment and a state budget that includes a large contribution from tobacco tax revenue, the long term societal cost of smoking vastly outweighs the short term gains.

References

1. World Health Organization [database on the Internet] [cited 2008 Jul 30] Available from: http://www.smokefreeengland.co.uk/files/who-euro.pdf.

2. European Health Interview Survey: Bulgaria (2008) [Internet] The European Health Surveys Information Database[Cited 2011 Sep 16]. Available from: https://hishes.iph.fgov.be.

3. CDC Press Release Slightly Lower Adult Smoking Rates. November 2008. Center for Disease Control and Prevention. Available from: http://www.cdc.gov/media/pressrel/2008/r081113.htm.

4. World Health Organization. World Health statistics 2010 Available from: http://www.who.int/whosis/whostat/EN_WHS10_Full.pdf).

5. Smoking prevalence varies widely among EU-27 member states. European Union Public Health Information System. (Access date: July 2007) Available from: http://www.euphix.org/object_document/o4748n27423.html.

6. Bulgarians Prepare for Smoking Ban. December 2009. CCTV. Available from: http://www.no-smoke.org/goingsmokefree.php?id=644.

7. Ministry Of Health (2001) National Health Strategy. Better health for a better future of Bulgaria.Sofia. Available from http://ec.europa.eu/health/ph_projects/1999/monitoring/bulgaria_en.pdf.

8. Green, L W. Taxes and the tobacco wars. Canadian Medical Association Journal. 1997 Jan 15; 156 (2): 205-206. In: ProQuest Health Management [database on the Internet] [cited 2008 Sep 21]. Available from: http://www.proquest.com/; Document ID: 418440181.

9. The European Tobacco Control Report. World Health Organization. Regional Office for Europe; 2007 [cited 2010 Dec. 9]. Available from http://www.euro.who.int/__data/assets/pdf_file/0005/68117/E89842.pdf.

10. Euromonitor International's Tobacco in Bulgaria market report. Available from: http://www.euromonitor.com/Tobacco_in_Bulgaria.

11. Eastern Europe: EU expansion offers opportunities and challenges. Source from: World Tobacco News article id: 13483; 28 January 2008. [Cited 2010 Dec. 12]. Available from http://act.tobaccochina.net/englishnew/content1.aspx?id=36723.

12. Tsoneva-Pentcheva L., Willmore I. Bulgaria: Conduit for Illicit Cigarette Trade between Asia and Europe. Framework Alliance Convention Bulletin. 2010 March; 97: 4.

13. Effective Policies Targeting the Corruption-Organized Crime Nexus in Bulgaria: Closing Down Duty-Free Outlets. (December 2007), No 13, Center for the Study of Democracy. Brief.

14. Corruption, Contraband and Organized Crime in Southeast Europe. Center for the Study of Democracy. Sofia (2003). Available from: http://unpan1.un.org/intradoc/groups/public/documents/untc/unpan016997.pdf.

15. Bakalov, I. Нещо се мъти с цигарите. От контрабандата се печели както никога. 22 December 2010. Available from: http://e-vestnik.bg/9972/neshto-se-mati-s-tsigarite-ot-kontrabandata-se-pecheli-kakto-nikoga/.

16. European Commission Directorate General Taxation and Customs Union. Excise Duty tables. Ref 1.031. July 2010. Available from: http://ec.europa.eu/taxation customs/index en.htm#.

17. Bulgaria Average Salary Up by 16.3% in First Quarter of 2009. Business. May 18, 2009. Available from http://www.novinite.com/view_news.php?id=103725.

18. Reporting Instrument- Bulgaria (December 2008). World Health Organization. WHO Framework Convention on Tobacco Control. Available from http://www.who.int/fctc/reporting/party_reports/bgr/en/index.html.

19. Eastern Europe: EU expansion offers opportunities and challenges. News article ID: 13483. 28 January, 2008. [Cited 2010 Dec. 22]. Available from http://act.tobaccochina.net/englishnew/content1. aspx?id=36723.

20. Euromonitor International's Tobacco in Bulgaria Market report. Available from: http//www.euromonitor.com/Tobacco_in_Bulgaria.

21. Petkova, R Yiridirak, N. Employment Trends in the Tobacco Sector: Selected Provinces of Bulgaria and Turkey. Working paper. International Labour Office. Geneva. 2003.

22. Report from the State of Bulgaria. Interactive European Network for Industrial Crops and Their Applications. Alexandra Balabanova. 2004.

23. Joossens, L. Raw, M. Progress in Tobacco Control in 30 European Countries, 2005-2007. Swiss Cancer League. Report presented at the 4th European Conference Tobacco or Health 2007, Basel, Switzerland, 11-13 October 2007.

24. European Commission, Public Health Tobacco Products Directive (2001/37/EC). Available from: http://www.who.int/whosis/whostat/ EN_WHS10_Full.pdf).

Romania

The tobacco culture was believed to have been brought to Romania by the Turks in the middle of the 16th century. Oriental, semi-oriental and burley tobacco are currently cultivated. As in the other Balkan countries, the habit of cigarette smoking was historically highly prevalent, socially acceptable and considered a sign of adulthood. In Romania smoking has a high social acceptance and Romanian youth often see teenagers and adults smoking. The common expectation in Romania is that youth will eventually smoke.

Smoking Prevalence

Romania, with a population of 21.9 million, is the largest market for cigarettes in South Eastern Europe. Data available from a 2007 survey found that the smoking prevalence in Romania was 31.0% (1). For comparison, an estimated 19.8 percent of U.S. adults were current smokers in 2007 (2). The prevalence of current tobacco smoking is an important predictor of the potential for future tobacco-related diseases. World Health Statistics 2010 reported that the prevalence of smoking any tobacco product among adults aged 15 years or older in 2006 was 49% for males and 38 % for females. This compares with 21.5% prevalence for males and 16.6% prevalence for females for the European region in general (3). There is a wide variation in smoking prevalence among EU 27 nations. The proportion of those aged 15 years and over who smoke in the EU-27 ranges from 16% in Sweden to 38% in Greece (4). The most recent comparable data for Romania is for 2009 and indicates that 33.7% of those aged 15 years and over smoke. (5). A study conducted in 2004 in 5 high schools in Romania showed that 11.8% of students aged 15-17 years smoked occasionally and 24.5% smoked constantly(6). Among health professionals, the percentage of smokers is even higher with a smoking prevalence of 43.2% (50.1% in men and 38.6% in women) among physicians (7). Of particular concern is that the young age group (24 to 34 years old) as a group reports some of the highest prevalence rates for daily smoking. Table 1 shows that the smoking prevalence in Romania is higher than the EU27 average of 31% adults smoking.

Table 1—Smoking Prevalence

Country	Smokers	Non-smokers	Ex-smokers	Never smoked
EU27	31%	68%	22%	46%
Romania	36%	64%	17%	47%
Bulgaria	39%	62%	17%	45%
Croatia	33%	67%	16%	51%
Hungary	36%	64%	19%	45%

Note: EU27-European Union Member States.

The percentages of smokers and non-smokers may not sum to 100 because of rounding.

Source: Eurobarometer : Survey on Tobacco Analytical Report, EC, 2009.
http://ec.europa.eu/public_opinion/flash/fl_253_en.pdf
Statistics for Croatia from Goel, R. K. & Budak, J. "Smoking Patterns in Croatia and Comparisons with European Nations." Central European Journal of Public Health 2007; 15 93): 110-115.

Non-price policies that have spawned anti-smoking regulation encompass a whole range of strategies including geographic restrictions, tobacco advertising bans, sales limitations, packaging mandates, and health warnings about tobacco consumption. Table 2 and 3 summarize the current non-price policies on tobacco products in Romania. Pricing policies to reduce tobacco consumption are essentially tax based policies. The use of tax based policies to reduce consumption in Romania are complex due to competing interests among tobacco executives, legislators, retailers and health professionals among others.

Table 2—Legislation on advertising and distribution of tobacco products in Romania

Description	Ban	Partial Restriction
Direct advertising of tobacco products		
National TV	X	
Cable TV	X	
National radio	X	
International TV	X	
International radio	X	
Local magazines, newspapers	X	
Billboards, outdoor walls	X	
Cinemas	X	
Indirect Advertising of tobacco products		
Sponsored events with tobacco brand name	X	
Promotional discounts	X	
Distribution of tobacco products through various outlets		
Sale of single or unpacked cigarettes	X	
Free samples of cigarettes (to minors only)	X	
Duty free shops	X	
Smoke- free areas		
Health care facilities	X	
Education facilities		X
Restaurants		X
Pubs and bars		X
Indoor workplaces and offices		X
Smoke-free public transit		
Buses	X	
Taxis	X	
Trains	X	
Domestic air transport	X	
International air transport	X	

Table 3—Legislation on health warnings, ingredients/
constituents, number of cigarettes per pack and
minimum age for buying tobacco.

Description	Required/ Regulated	Comments
Minimum age for buying tobacco products	X	18 years
Health warnings on tobacco products:	X	
Ensuring that hatch warnings are rotating	X	
Color, contrast, font size	X	
Area to cover	X	Not less than 30% of principal display area
Language	X	
Pictorial warnings	X	
Disclosure of ingredient or constituent information:		
To government	X	
On packages	X	

Source: Romanian Reporting Instrument to the European Union.

Pricing policies to control tobacco consumption

Tax increases are the most effective intervention to persuade people who are acutely price sensitive to quit or not to start smoking. Young people and many low income Romanians tend to be highly sensitive to price increases. Although there is no conclusive data on the impact of pricing policies on cigarette consumption in Romania, experience from another Eastern European country, Hungary, found that regular tobacco tax increases resulted in decreased cigarette consumption and lower prevalence figures in some population groups (8). Raising taxes on tobacco products is considered one of the most important strategies for tobacco control.

As elsewhere in the Balkans, cigarette tax is composed of excise tax, ad valorem tax (levied as a percentage of price) and value added tax. According to data from the World Health Organization, the structure of taxation for tobacco products (%) 2006 for Romania is as follows:

Specific excise	22.72
Ad valorem excise	30.00
VAT	19.00
Total tax	71.72

Romanian cigarettes are still less expensive than elsewhere in Europe. Although Romania increased excise duties in 2009, they continue to lag behind other European areas in its use of a taxing strategy to combat smoking. Cigarette taxes in Romania have not been increased as much as desirable because government officials fear the economy will be adversely impacted by reduced employment and income. The fear is that demand may decrease so much that the increase in revenue resulting from the tax increases will be offset by reduced sales volumes.

The major tobacco companies in Romania are transnational. State owned companies have been privatized or closed. The most recognized and best selling local brands of cigarettes in Romania are Snagov, Ronson, and Carpati.

Table 4 shows the price of a pack of cigarettes* in Romania for the most popular foreign and Romanian brands (2010).

Table 4—Prices per pack of cigarettes* in Romania for the most popular foreign and local brands in 2010

Foreign brands	Price (€)	Romanian brands	Price (€)
Marlboro	5.7 Lei (1.34 €)	Snagov	4.2 Lei (.98 €)
Pall Mall	5.3 Lei (1.24 €)	Ronson	4.7 Lei (1.10€)
Camel	5.7 Lei (1.34€)	Carpati	4. Lei (.94 €)

*20 cigarettes per pack. Prices include taxes

Preferences for cigarette brands are nationally determined. The most popular domestic cigarette in Romania is the Snagov brand at 4.2 lei per pack. This can be compared to a kilogram of apples at 2.39 lei, one loaf of white bread at 2.50 lei, 10 eggs at 3.69 lei, or a ½ liter bottle of local beer (Timisoreana) at 5 lei. The Euorostat –OECD Purchasing Power Parity Program produces data on price relatives that show the ratio of the prices in national currencies of the same goods or services in different countries. Price level indices (PLIs) provide a comparison of the countries' PLI with respect to the European Union average: if the price level index is higher than 100, the country concerned is relatively expensive compared to the EU 27 average and vice versa. The EU average is calculated as the weighted average of the national PLIs, weighted with the expenditures corrected for price level differences. Price levels for tobacco vary considerably in the EU countries. This data indicates that tobacco in Romania is relatively cheap compared to surrounding countries and other foods and beverages. The PLI for tobacco in Romania is the lowest of all the EU27 countries. In 2009, the PLI for tobacco in Romania was 47 compared to food (65 PLI) and alcoholic beverages (70 PLI) (9). Country comparisons show that cigarettes in Romania are relatively affordable, particularly given the availability of smuggled cigarettes which can be bought even more cheaply.

Smuggling

Corruption and organized crime are linked to cigarette smuggling and are perceived by the public to be widespread in Romania. The EU still cites Romania as being one of the most corrupt countries in the EU. Organized crime, particularly the type which relates to trafficking of smuggled cigarettes has turned into one of the most important mechanism for unlawful redistribution of national wealth. The smuggling of goods is an important source of income for various groups ranging from political leaders, government officials, and people living in border areas. In fact, Romanian police have recently arrested 59 customs officials and border police on charges of taking bribes and involvement in cigarette smuggling.

Cigarettes represent perhaps the most popular item for smuggling in Romania due to their small size, high price, very large consumption and high import tax rates. The illicit trade volume of cigarettes sold in Romania increased significantly over the course of 2010. The reason is the increase in the value added tax to 24% and wage cuts in the public sector (10). Some schools of thought believe the effectiveness of tax policies is undermined to the extent there are smuggled or counterfeit tobacco products on the market. Smuggled cigarettes are less expensive because taxes and duties are not paid. In fact, tobacco companies argue that increased taxation is an incentive for smuggling. Additionally, smuggling allows international brands to become affordable to low income consumers and to image conscious young people in developing countries. Young people in Romania regard international brands as sophisticated and stylish. Recent experience in Romania suggests that tax hikes while leading to a decrease in sales of cigarettes has also led to an increase in black market cigarettes. In Romania, cigarettes are widely available on the black market and producers estimate cigarette contraband will account for almost 30% of the total market in 2010 (11).

Many goods that are smuggled undergo transformation or like tobacco and alcohol, are consumed. This makes the tracking of smuggled goods more difficult. Cigarettes are high import tax items which make them especially appealing for smugglers and consumers alike. Tobacco companies have little incentive to reduce smuggling as lower priced cigarettes contribute to consumption. Tobacco companies sell cigarettes whether they are taxed or not. The common scheme for smuggling locally produced cigarettes usually involves "export" to a neighboring country, followed by illegal transport back into the country of origin. Most contraband cigarettes sold in Romania come from the Republic of Moldova (31.5%), Ukraine (24%) and Serbia (21.7%). Overall, the three countries account for 77% of the total contraband market. (12)

Map of Romania

Methods used to smuggle cigarettes into Romania include hiding cigarettes among food transported in refrigerated trucks, in metal pipes, in lorries carrying wheat, in private cars, in mattresses, in wooden toys, in wheel rims, and by foot across the borders. Individuals who smuggle by foot across the border between Romania and Ukraine are paid 35 to 50 Euros for each crossing. Smuggling in Romania is further facilitated by its 245 kilometer long coast line on the Black Sea which is difficult to patrol. In general, coastline on the Black Sea is more difficult to patrol than land borders. Due to high import taxes and duty rates, smuggling cigarettes can be a profitable activity. Smugglers arbitrage the differences between lower- and-higher countries. For example, there are huge differences between the price of cigarettes in the Ukraine and the European Union. In addition to smuggled cigarettes the incidence of counterfeit cigarettes continues to diversify and grow in Romania. A recent prosecution in the UK noted that Romania was a transit site for counterfeit cigarettes destined to the United Kingdom from Moldova and the Ukraine. These cigarettes generally contain low grade tobacco and excessive levels of nicotine.

Statistics of cigarette smuggling are difficult to locate as the topic does not easily lend itself to being a topic of academic scrutiny. The volume of cigarette smuggling in Romania can in part be measured by the amount of cigarettes seized by customs officials. Although admittedly, this can also be a measure of the rigor of policing efforts. In the first quarter of March 2010, the authorities confiscated 42 million cigarettes which were double the amount seized during the same period in 2008 (13). One study by a local company estimated that smuggled cigarettes accounted for 24.4% of the Romanian cigarette market in 2010 (14). A recent report in the popular Romanian press notes that smuggling in Romania has decreased in 2011 but there is no available source to verify this statement. Officially published estimates for the proportion of cigarettes smuggled do not exist.

To combat illicit trade, legislation needs to include measures such as requirements for cigarette package markings or creation of a computerized system for conclusively tracking and monitoring products through the entire channel of distribution. A specific intra-country task force and more stringent border control especially between Romania and Serbia may be needed to address this problem. Transparent prosecution of border patrols and customs officials who enable smuggling should be a high priority. Reductions in tobacco smuggling in Romania will also require a change in attitude. Smuggling is commonly perceived as a "soft" crime with no victims and no penalty.

Improvements are occurring. Romania has recently made efforts to increase the penalties for smuggling by authorizing the confiscation of vehicles used for smuggling. Romania is not alone in terms of its issues with cigarette smuggling. The United States also has a problem with cigarette smuggling. State tax revenues are losing about $5 billion annually because of illegal tobacco sales (15). Indeed, a study conducted by Lovenheim (2008) estimated that the percent of consumers who smuggle is between 13 percent and 25 percent nationwide (16). Other scholars have advanced similar estimates.

Unemployment

In the late 1940s Romania, like Bulgaria and Yugoslavia, was under Soviet influence and considered itself a socialist country. From 1967 to 1989 Romania was under a totalitarian single party state ruled by the communist dictator Nicolae Ceausescu. Due to Ceausescu's personality, the Romanian revolution has been characterized as the bloodiest of the eastern European economic transitions. Since 1990, Romania's political landscape and government have dramatically changed. Today there are free elections and the country is currently a parliamentary democracy that includes conservatives, social democrats and communist parties. Romania was the first country of Central and Eastern Europe to have official relations with the European Community and officially joined the EU in 2007. After the collapse of the communist regime, the country experienced a long and challenging transition period in the 1990's with severe changes in the labor market. Under the previous communist regime, unemployment was virtually non-existent due to pronounced job security. Romania's painful but largely successful transition from a rigid centrally planned economic system to market-oriented capitalism has produced an economic and social upheaval. The transition to a market economy initially resulted in a high jobless rate, increasing inequality of incomes, and de-industrialization. Although showing signs of recent improvement and a viable market system, unemployment is a burning topic for the current center-right government, irrespective of the considerable differences in data about unemployment in various official sources. In 2009, the tobacco industry was one of the biggest state budget contributors providing over 2 billion Euros from VAT and other taxes (17) in addition to providing employment.

Romania has favorable climate conditions for the cultivation of the basic blends that compose almost all cigarette types but compared to its neighbors cultivates a relatively small tobacco crop of low quality. Romania has approximately 10,970 hectares of land devoted to growing tobacco or 1% of its agricultural land. For comparison, its neighbor to the south, Bulgaria, devotes 42,000 hectares to growing tobacco and Moldova to the east devotes 18,608 hectares (18). Romania does devote an economic effort to the manufacturing of cigarettes. The cigarette category in Romania is now completely privatized with multinationals accounting for 98% of retail volume in 2009 (19). Tobacco constitutes an important sector of manufacturing and an industry which contributes heavily to the national budget. In terms of exports, cigarettes accounted for 1% of the volume of Romanian exports in 2010 (20). As smoke-free policies motivate some smokers to give up smoking, there may be a loss of profit to the tobacco industry and, consequently, reductions in tobacco-related employment. Among EU members, Romania is the second poorest member with an unemployment rate of 8.4 %, declining exports, and a commitment to the International Monetary Fund to lower its budget deficit to 5.9% of gross domestic product. (21).

Taxation

The leading international tobacco companies in Romania are British American Tobacco (BAT), Altria Group, Inc. and Japan Tobacco Inc. in that order (22). Cigarette tax is a very important source of government revenue in Eastern Europe and in Romania in particular. These three major companies provided the state with over 2 billion euro in 2009, from VAT and other taxes (23). In addition to the large international tobacco companies, JBS Trade SRL, Imperial Tobacco Group Plc, Chinese producer Sinoroma Industry and a few other smaller manufacturers also contribute tax revenue to the state budget.

Romanian cigarette preferences in recent years have moved from traditionally inexpensive, low-quality cigarettes to more expensive products.

In 2010, the price for a pack of cigarettes in Romania almost doubled due to higher taxes and fees imposed by the state. The target goal is to reach the taxation and pricing levels seen in the European Union to discourage illegal trade. Despite all the tax increases, the price stayed at one-half to two-thirds of the average price per pack in Europe (24).

The majority of tobacco that is produced in Romania is produced by small family (lineal) farms concentrated in areas where there are few economic opportunities. The provinces of Walachia, Transylvania, Moldavia, Dobruja, and the Banat have the soil and climatic conditions that make them most suitable for agriculture (25). Family farms receive state support and produce tobacco on a contract basis. Tobacco production employs more labor hours per hectare than other crops such as cereals. These tobacco growers contribute to the national employment rate in a country that is working hard to stimulate its economy. National public health goals to decrease smoking consumption versus the desire for a financially robust economy contribute to the push/pull of a healthy population versus economic stability and growth. Still, taxation remains a powerful tool, particularly in the young, to discourage smoking. Additional taxation with revenues earmarked specifically for public health efforts aimed at smoking cessation could be imposed.

Conclusion

Since Romania joined the European Union, it has experienced rapid economic development. However, this has not always been the case with health care in general and smoking cessation efforts in particular. On 27 January 2006, Romania ratified the WHO Framework Convention on Tobacco Control. Progress on health reforms related to tobacco control in Romania has been mixed. On a positive note, Romania joined the group of countries offering comprehensive help to quit smoking in 2008. (26).

The Romanian population has access to toll-free quit lines and nicotine replacement therapy is available in pharmacies without a prescription.

Underlying tobacco control policies is eliminating tobacco smoke to create a 100% smoke free environment. In most countries the creation of smoke free environments has proven to be one of the most effective and popular tobacco control interventions. One hundred percent smoke free legislation not only reduces the hazardous health effects of exposure to tobacco smoke but it 'denormalizes" smoking habits, resulting in many people quitting (27). While smoking is banned in educational facilities, hospitals, and public transit, smoking in restaurants is still widely prevalent.

A positive development was that 1 % of tobacco and excise duties were to be used to finance national programs on tobacco alcohol and drugs from 2007 to 2010. (28). Reliable data on how this 1% was actually spent is not, however, readily available.

On paper and in public health rhetoric, Romania has accepted and embraced the modern concept of health promotion, which aims to improve the level of public health by tackling health determinants and not just preventing disease. A much stronger and consistent effort aimed at the entire smoking population is needed to encourage individuals to stop smoking. Ideally, action should include age, ethnic, and gender-based promotional and educational programs. Maternity, drug abuse, and mental health centers should be a regular site for smoking intervention programs. Romania does have local accredited standards available for smoking cessation training but it is not monitored by the country. Treatment for smokers who would like to quit should be provided either at reduced cost or free of charge. Training in smoking cessation should be part of the basic curriculum for all health professionals. Even brief and simple advice from health professionals can have a substantial increase in smoking cessation rates. A primary focus of all primary health care providers (nurses, physicians, dentists and pharmacists) should be efforts and education about smoking cessation. In general, primary care providers in Romania are over-worked, poorly paid and deal more commonly with acute illness or exacerbation of chronic ones than in preventative medicine. Placing a stronger emphasis on smoking cessation efforts will be a major challenge given the recent cuts to the Health Minister's budget, physician strikes, widespread physician bribery, and crumbling hospital physical plants.

The regulation regarding smoking in public places and the workplace should become more restrictive and there is the outstanding issue of effective enforcement of existing regulations. Violations of smoking in public areas are a common, customary, and acceptable occurrence. Current regulation should be enforced particularly in educational and governmental facilities with very heavy penalties and when disputes arise, litigation should be pursued. Sanitation inspectors who oversee the implementation of the regulation could provide regular automatic reports to the Minister of Health on adherence violations and the action taken. Smoking should be banned in all public places including restaurants, pubs, bars and public transportation. As elsewhere in the Balkans, restaurant, café, and bar owners loudly protest this effort citing a major negative effect on their revenues. Ashtrays which are commonly found on tables in restaurants and cafes evidence lack of enforcement. Further, social marketing efforts should stress non smokers' rights to enjoy a smoke free environment so that individuals will be less tolerant of public exposure to second hand smoke.

Additional efforts are needed with respect to the advertising of tobacco. Tobacco advertising was predominant in Timisoara Romania. In 2003, Timisoara was the first Romanian city to be free of tobacco advertising. Tobacco companies sued the local council and after 9 months regained the right to advertise. It is suggested that legislation be enacted to ban advertising at point of sale, and kiosks. Regarding promotion, sponsorship, and all forms of indirect advertising, the country would be wise to adopt a total ban on advertising.

In Romania, smoking hazards are outlined in direct health warning labels on cigarette boxes. One side of the box says "Fumatul poate să ucidă" (Smoking might kill) and the other side says "Fumatul dăunează grav sănătății tale și a celor din jur" (Smoking harms your health and that of the people around you).

Cigarette warning label in Romanian:
"Smoking might kill"

Effective procedures regulating the packaging and labeling of tobacco products are a key component of a comprehensive tobacco control strategy. Requiring large, graphic health warnings is among the demand reduction measures recommended by the WHO. Since 2004, it has been possible to accompany such warnings with a picture. Pictorial health warnings on the two main sides of tobacco products would serve to strengthen the health warning. Evidence for the greater potential impact of pictorial warnings have come from focus groups and interview studies, experimental exposure studies and population-based surveys among Canadian smokers, Australian youth, and Dutch smokers (29). Large comprehensive graphic warnings that combine a picture and a text message relevant to the depicted picture have been shown to be effective in increasing adult awareness of the dangers of smoking (30,31,32). To their credit, Romania is one of three European Union countries (Belgium, United Kingdom, and Romania) to include pictures to motivate users to quit and to make tobacco less attractive to young people. They effected this change in 2008.

A desirable strategy would be one that includes raising cigarette taxes to EU levels, a complete ban of smoking in public places, enforcing the laws against selling tobacco to children, and offering free or inexpensive help to smokers trying to quit. Tobacco farm subsidies in any form should be eliminated. Historically tobacco is a highly desirable crop for farmers providing a higher net income yield per acre than other cash crops and most food crops. Alternative crops, while not as profitable would be revenue producers if subsidized. Price supports and subsidies for tobacco make little sense in the current climate. Finally, an economic package that stimulates the economy and reduces the burden of unemployment will do much to help close the gap between those who feel the need for tobacco revenues and those who place a higher value on individual human life.

As it enters the twenty first century, Romania is in the midst of a robust rebound. The economic prospect is optimistic given an increase in foreign investment, its current progress with new business ventures, increases in industrial production and its yet untapped potential for tourism in the Carpathian Mountain region. In many areas, Romania can be viewed as an advancing country. The public health sector is one area that needs increased emphasis. Placing a high value on and preserving the health of its citizens is consistent with a forward thinking country whose goal is to be a fully integrated European country. Although this is a challenge for a young democratic government with high unemployment and a state budget that includes a large contribution from tobacco tax revenue, the long term societal cost of smoking vastly outweighs the short term gains.

References

1. Center of health policies and Studies. Knowledge, Attitudes and Practices of the General Population on the Consumption of Tobacco and the legislative Provisions. 2007. Romania: Bucuresti. Available from: http://www.ms.ro/fisiere/pagini_virtuale/284_578_StudiuCPSS_07complet.pdf.

2. CDC Press Release Slightly Lower Adult Smoking Rates. November 2008. Center for Disease Control and Prevention. Available from: http://www.cdc.gov/media/pressrel/2008/r081113.htm

3. World Health Organization. World Health Statistics 2010 Available from: http://www.who.int/whosis/whostat/EN_WHS10_Full.pdf).

4. Smoking prevalence varies widely among EU-27 member states. European Union Public Health Information System. (Access date: July 2007) Available from: http://www.euphix.org/object_document/o4748n27423.html.

5. Eurobarometer 72.3 European Commission. Available from: http://ec.europa.eu/public_opinion/archives/ebs/ebs_332_fact_ro_en.pdf.

6. Lotrean, L., Ionut, C., & De Vries, H. "Why Do Romanian Adolescents Smoke?" The 13th World Conference on Tobacco OR Health. July 12-15, 2006. Washington, DC, USA.

7. Didilescu, C. & Munteanu, I. (2000) The Prevalence of Smoking in physicians in Romania. Pneumologia 49 (2):91-94.

8. Szilágyi-Tibor. Higher cigarette taxes-healthier people, wealthier state: the Hungarian experience. Cent. Eur J Public Health. 2007 Sep; 15 (3):122-6.

9. Kurkowiak, B. "Price levels for food, beverages and tobacco across the European market differ significantly". Economy and Finance. Eurostat. Statistics in Focus. 30/2010.

10. Cigarette Smuggling in Romania on Upward Trend in Sept, To 24.4% of Overall Market. Medifax. November 24, 2010. Available

from: http://site.securities.com/doc.html?pc=Ro&print=1&doc_id
=286328497&query=cigaret.

11.   Cigarette Smuggling in Romania at 24.4% of Overall Market in Sept
      Survey. Act Media Daily bulletin. Emerging Markets Information
      Service. October 22, 2010. Available from: http://www.mediafax.ro/
      english/cigarette-smuggling-in-romania-at-24-4-of-overall-market-in-
      sept-survey-7517360.

12.   Seenews (BG) Smuggling to Feed One-third of Romania's 2010
      Cigarette Market. October 21, 2010. Available from: http://www.
      tobacco.org/articles/country/romania/.

13.   Munteanu, M. Romania Cracks Down on Tobacco Smugglers. Financial
      Times. London. March 12, 2010.

14.   Cigarette Smuggling in Romania at 24.4% of Overall Market in Sept
      Survey. Act Media Daily bulletin. Emerging Markets Information
      Service. October 22, 2010. Available from: http://www.mediafax.ro/
      english/cigarette-smuggling-in-romania-at-24-4-of-overall-market-in-
      sept-survey-7517360.

15.   Fields, Gary. States Go to War on Cigarette Smuggling. The Wall Street
      Journal. July 20, 2009.

16.   Lovenheim, Michael. How Far to the Border: The extent of Cross-
      Border Casual Cigarette Smuggling. National Tax Journal.   March
      2008.

17.   Cracking down cigarette smuggling would get Romania EUR 1 bln.
      Romania needs that bln! Nine O'clock May 4, 2010. Available from:
      www.tobacco.org/news/301045.html.

18.   Mackay, Judith & Erikson, Michael. WHO Tobacco Atlas Available
      from: http://www.int/tobacco/statistics/tobacco-atlas/en/print.html.

19.   Euromonitor International 2009. Sector Capsule: Cigarettes-Romania.
      November 5, 2010. Available from: www.euromonitor.com.

20. Mihai, Adelina. Philip Morris exports 95m euro's worth of cigarettes, JTI 35% of its output. Ziarul Financiar. January 20, 2011.

21. Savu, Irina. Romania's Unemployment Rose to a Seven -Year High in March. Bloomberg Business Week. April 8, 2010. Available from: http://www.businessweek.com/news/2010-04-08/romania-s-unemployment-rate-rose-to-seven-year-high-in-march.html.

22. Datamonitor. Tobacco in Romania to 2011.   Available from http://www.reportlinker.com/p060342/Tobacco-in--Romania-to.html.

23. ENTdesign Cracking down cigarette smuggling would get Romania EUR 1 bln. Romania needs that bln! Nine O'Clock (ro), May 4, 2010. Available from: http://www.tobacco.org/articles/country/romania/.

24. Tobacco in Romania. Euoromonitor International. November 2010. Available from: http://www.euromonitor.com/Tobacco_in_Romania.

25. Bachman, R. D., ed. Romania: A Country Study. Washington: GPO for the Library of Congress. 1989. Available from: http://countrystudies.us/romania/.

26. WHO Tobacco Control Country profiles. 2nd edition, 2003. Available from: http://www.who.int/tobacco/media/en/Romania.pdf.

27. WHO Report on the Global Tobacco Epidemic, 2009. WHO. Available from: http://whqlibdoc.who.int/publications/2009/9789241563918_eng_full.pdf.

28. Bostic C. (Ed.) Tobacco Watch: Monitoring Countries Performance on the Tobacco Treaty. Geneva. Framework Convention Alliance. 2010.

29. Fong, G, Hammond, D & Hitchman, S. The impact of pictures on the effectiveness of tobacco warnings. Bulletin of the World Health Organization. 2009; 87:640-643.

30. Hammond D, Fong G, McNeil A. et al. Text Effectiveness of cigarette warning labels in informing smokers about the risks of smoking. Findings from the International Tobacco control four country survey. Tobacco Control 2006a; 15:19-i25.

31. Hammond D, Fong G, Borland R. et al. Text and Graphic warnings on cigarette packages. Findings from the International Tobacco Control Four Countries Study. Am j Prev Med 2007; 32:202-9.

32. O'Hegarty M, Pederson L, nelson D, et al. Reactions of young adult smokers to warning labels on cigarette packages. Am J Prev Med 2006; 30:467-73.

Greece

Greece is politically, culturally and economically different from the previously discussed three countries. It was firmly on the side of the west during the cold war, while the other three countries were part of "Eastern Europe" (as in "Communist" Europe). Economically, Greece has always been a capitalist economy with a dominant service sector (shipping and tourism are by far the largest contributors to the country's gross domestic product). Greece joined the OECD in 1961 and the European Union in 1981. At that time it was deemed to have met the requirement that it have a functioning market economy as well as the capacity to cope with competitive pressure and market forces within the Union. Much has changed for Greece since its acceptance into the EU.

Currently, Greece is a capitalist economy with a parliamentary democracy. Up until 2008, Greece was enjoying one of the highest growth rates in Europe. The economy went into recession in 2009 as a result of the world financial crisis, tightening credit conditions, and failure to address a growing budget deficit. This deficit was triggered by falling state revenues and increased public spending. Financing costs for Greece rose rapidly, adding to the already high debt burden. Loans and financial assistance were provided by the EU and recent austerity measures have reduced the deficit as a percentage of GDP. Public debt, inflation, and unemployment are still above the euro-zone average while per capita income is a little below. The government has adopted an austerity program that includes cutting government spending, reducing the size of the public sector, and decreasing tax evasion. The government's program also includes reform to such crucial sectors as tax administration, the labor market, and the health sector. The most severe consequences of this crisis are borne by ordinary Greek citizens. The Greek unemployment rate is 30.4% among those who are 20 to 24 years old (1). Business is down, sales are slow, prices are higher for food and heating oil and most people have little discretionary money.

Reforming the health care system can have implications for tobacco control measures. The public health care system in Greece provides free, or low cost, healthcare services to residents (and their families) contributing to the social security system. The current health care system is full of debt, plagued with corruption, seriously overdue in payment to pharmaceutical firms, and crippled by inefficiencies. The health care system is so endemic with bribery that the Greeks have a special word for the envelopes of cash that is given to physicians- "fakelaki". A proposal exists in Greece to create a fresh institutional framework for the provision of primary care which is designed to give patients wider access to practitioners, to solve chronic delays and improve service quality. Endeavors of this kind are not guaranteed. If greater access to health care professionals is available it could be assumed that smoking cessation efforts would be increased but the ultimate effect this revised system will have on issues such as smoking prevalence is not known.

Map of Greece

Smoking prevalence in Greece

Greece has a pro-tobacco culture and smoking proliferates. Smoking is something Greeks enjoy and is deeply embedded in their social relationships. According to the Greek Reporting Instrument to the World Health Organization for the period 2006-2008, the prevalence of smoking for males and females is 38% (2). Currently Greece has the highest smoking prevalence not only among members of the European Union but also among all members of the OECD (3).

Adolescents in Greece have a major smoking problem. Although recent nationwide smoking research is scarce, smoking prevalence among adolescents and young adults is high. Smoking prevalence ranged from 10% to 32% for 15 year olds depending on the location. (4, 5). Even in health care service centers, smoking is evident. Vardavas et al (2009) looked at the smoking habits of health care personnel in the University Hospital of Crete, which is located in

Heraklion, Greece. They found that hospital staff is characterized by elevated smoking rates of both physicians and nursing staff, with the highest prevalence found among the latter (6). This speaks to the lack of role models for tobacco control efforts among health care professionals towards patients and society.

In addition to the health problems that are caused as a direct result of smoking, tobacco workers also suffer serious illnesses from constant handling of the tobacco leaves. Illnesses include contact dermatitis, green tobacco sickness (GTS), and musculo-skeletal injuries from repetitive movements and awkward posture. In Greece, they are given special benefits and retire earlier than other workers.

Anti-smoking legislation

Anti-smoking policies do exist in Greece. A lack of enforcement and widespread public rebelliousness is being blamed for the Greeks' inability to conform to European standards regarding smoking. Indeed cigarettes and coffee are almost a national symbol in Greece. The picture is actually much more complicated than this.

Greece has significant legislation to control smoking. Since older legislation was not very efficient, a new stricter law was passed. Effective in 2010, the law bans smoking and consumption of tobacco products by other means, in all working places, transportation stations, in taxis and passenger ships (in trains, buses and airplanes smoking is already prohibited), as well as in all enclosed public places including restaurants, night clubs, etc., without any exception. Under this legislation, individuals can be fined up to 300 euros for smoking in enclosed public places. According to Vardavas and Kafatos (2007) smoke-free environments in Greece are scarce. Despite existent legislation that forbids smoking in all educational institutes, environmental tobacco smoke is evident in establishments from primary schools to university campuses, mainly because of the non-compliance of teachers, staff, and students. Even health-care services are not always smoke-free despite being declared to be so since 2002 (7). Passing laws banning smoking is the first step but enforcing it is another. The law is ineffectively enforced in Greece.

Greece ratified the WHO Framework Convention on Tobacco Control on 27 January 2006. By signing this international act, they have stated their consent to be bound by it. This United Nations treaty was negotiated under the auspices of the World Health Organization and is one of the most successful treaties dedicated to protecting the health of the public through decreasing tobacco consumption. Their first implementation report was submitted on 7 October 2008. The following information is extracted from that report.

Legislation on advertising and distribution of tobacco products in Greece is summarized in Table 1.

Table 1—Select Legislation on advertising and distribution of tobacco products in Greece

Description	Yes	No
Instituting a comprehensive ban of all tobacco advertising, promotion and sponsorship?		X
Prohibiting all forms of tobacco advertising, promotion and sponsorship that promote a tobacco product by any means that are false, misleading, deceptive or likely to create an erroneous impression?		X
Requiring that health or other appropriate warnings or messages accompany all tobacco advertising and promotion and sponsorship?	X	
Restricting the use of direct or indirect incentives that encourage the purchase of tobacco products by the public?		X
Requiring the disclosure to relevant governmental authorities of expenditures by the tobacco industry on advertising, promotion and sponsorship not yet prohibited?		X
Restricting tobacco advertising, promotion and sponsorship on radio, television, print media and other media, such as the Internet?	X	
Prohibiting or restricting tobacco sponsorship of international events, activities and/or participants therein?	X	
Requiring that packaging and labeling contains information on relevant constituents and emissions of tobacco products?	X	
Requiring that the warnings and other textual information appear on each unit package, and on any outside packaging and labeling.	X	
Ensuring that the health warnings are in the form of, or include, pictures or pictograms?		X
Ensuring that the health warnings are rotating?	X	

Source: *Greece Reporting Instrument to the European Union. September 15, 2008.*
Submitted by Department of Public Health, Ministry of Health & Social Solidarity

In 2010 the government outlawed cigarette smoking in enclosed public spaces and placed new limits on tobacco advertising. This came after eight years of changes in the country's smoke free provisions, including a 2009 law that contained some exemptions and that was not widely enforced.

Under the new regulations, anyone who breaks the rules by smoking indoors in public will face fines of between €50 and €400. Business owners could be fined up to €10,000 or lose their licenses. Previous laws were largely ignored by the public and their failure was blamed on too many exceptions, lax policing and a reluctance to impose fines. Showing very positive signs of governmental solidarity among ministries, there was a joint ministerial decision signed by Ministers of Health, Finance, Interior, Citizen Protection, Labour and Culture and Tourism about the control procedures of the smoking ban. Those charged with enforcing the law are public health inspectors, the coast guard and municipal police. An additional 800 state inspectors were added in 2011 to increase checks on the enforcement of the smoking ban. Additionally, a campaign was initiated that included an advertising blitz accompanied by the distribution of anti-smoking board games to children.

The issue of smoking in enclosed public spaces is less problematic in the warm weather months (March through November). Greece is very much a café culture and much of the smoking is done outside during the warmer months.

The more stringent rules have raised complaints from smokers and bar and restaurant owners alike. Individual freedom and authoritarian defiance is a highly valued concept in Greece and whether this regulation can be successfully enforced is not yet known. Still, ash trays regularly appear alongside no smoking signs on tables in restaurants in Thessaloniki and elsewhere in Greece. The ban appears to be partly on paper at this point.

Interestingly, the ban that was enacted in the spring of 2009 was introduced by the center-right government and people in Greece were very defiant. The same law was reintroduced by the Socialist (center-left) government and compliance increased.

There is a general tendency among Greeks to be more agreeable to measures introduced by the socialists as opposed to the right-center government. The media were influential in this regard. When the former New Democracy government introduced the smoking ban all private TV channels interviewed only heavy smokers who were irate at the proposal and thus influenced public opinion. When the Panhellenic Socialist Movement (PASOK) government introduced the exact same measure the same media interviewed public health opinion in favor of the measure. Much of Greek opinion is influenced by party politics.

No Smoking Sign in Greece

There appears to be little awareness among adolescents of the health risks of second hand smoke (SHS). In semi-structured qualitative interviews with 14 to 16 year olds in Greece, Tamvakas and Amos (2010) described social worlds in which smoking and exposure to SHS was perceived to be both an inherent part of socializing and highly addictive. The 'right' to smoke in public places was viewed as greater than that of not being exposed to SHS and as normal and acceptable (8). In a related area, adolescents in Greece surveyed about health warnings on cigarette packs indicate that the proposed EU graphic warning labels would be more effective in preventing smoking and more effective in informing them about the health effects of smoking, in comparison to the existing EU text-only warnings (9). At this time, Greece does not employ pictorial warnings.

Tobacco production

As in other Balkan countries, tobacco constitutes an important sector of agriculture and industry which contributes heavily to the national budget. As smoke-free policies motivate some smokers to give up smoking, there may be a loss of profit to the tobacco industry and, consequently, reductions in tobacco-related employment. Among EU members, Greece is particularly vulnerable in this area with a high unemployment rate of 15.8% as of April 2011(10). The argument that reducing tobacco production will further exacerbate unemployment levels of Greek citizens may only be partially valid. Immigrants make up nearly one-fifth of the work force, mainly in agricultural and unskilled jobs. Many of the tobacco agricultural workers, particularly in the prefecture of Pieria are Albanian and Bulgarian immigrants.

Greece also is a major producer of tobacco in Europe. Tobacco grows well in Greece as it is strong growing plant with a strong resistance to heat and drought. In terms of proportion of total EU agricultural output of tobacco, Greece produces more than any other country. In 2001, Greece produced 130 thousand metric tons of tobacco leaves putting it in the top 10 countries in the world for tobacco production (11). Although tobacco production has fallen in the past few years as a result of "decoupling" of EU premiums in 2007, tobacco remains a significant agricultural product for Greece. Although Greece's leaf tobacco industry has been reduced in size, it offers a good quality product that is in demand by an international trade. The largest part of tobacco leaves processed and transported by most of the tobacco trading enterprises is sold abroad and primarily to well-known multinational companies producing cigarettes. The rest is sold to Greek cigarette manufacturers. Fourteen companies operate in Greece selling some 100 brands and 265 blends. In addition to local companies, the multinational companies have a strong presence in Greece. The tobacco companies in Greece are generally very vibrant. In May 2009, Philip Morris International (PMI) opened a new factory in Aspropyrgos representing a 100 million euro investment. PMI also has a tobacco warehouse facility in Agrinio and regional sales offices in Thessaloniki, Patras and Iraklio in Crete. PMI has approximately 800 employees in Greece. British American Tobacco (BAT) and Japan Tobacco International (JTI) also have a presence in Greece. Imperial Tobacco Hellas (ITH) is a subsidiary of Imperial Tobacco Group, a leading international tobacco company. During the past ten years, ITH has been the fastest-growing tobacco company in Greece, both in terms of volume and value. The company has achieved consistent, double-digit growth and more than doubled its market share during the past decade. In 2010 ITH was listed as one of "the Strongest Companies in Greece."

In Greece as well as other Balkan countries, public health officials seem to be at odds with the group that places an emphasis on the contribution of the tobacco industry to tax revenues and values the livelihood of people who make their living from growing or selling tobacco. Tobacco industries generally portray themselves as indispensable to the economy, arguing that tobacco creates employment, raises tax revenues, and contributes to the gross domestic product. Because the Greek economy is having financial difficulties, such arguments are difficult to argue against.

This pressure may in some measure be offset by pressures from the EU to use increased taxation on cigarettes, alcohol, and petrol as one strategy to assist with resolving the debt crisis.

However, the long-term societal costs of tobacco usage far outweigh any economic benefits. Since the statistics are so compelling that even passive smoking is harmful, it is baffling how any serious politician in Greece can now deny the evidence.

Smuggling

Migrants, artifacts and antiquities, fuel, alcohol and tobacco are all smuggled in Greece. The country is very interesting when it comes to cigarette smuggling. Apart from the fact that research on the topic in the country is in an embryonic state, Greece has a large smoking population, a significant black market economy, low "tax consciousness," and neighboring countries with large informal economies. In times of economic crisis such as Greece is experiencing more consumers tend to revert to the gray markets (parallel imports) due to their tighter budgets and decline in discretionary income.

Another interesting aspect about smuggling in Greece is that strong control of the land borders leads to an increase of illicit activities along the sea border. Greece has a long irregular coastline with the Adriatic Sea and over 2000 islands. Controlling smuggling along the sea is more difficult than controlling land smuggling. In 2010, smuggled cigarettes cost the state budget 88,413,394 euros in unpaid excise tax (12).

A study by Antounopolous (2007) has been able to provide a picture of the social organization of cigarette smuggling in Greece based on the available evidence. He suggests that Greece is a source, transit *and* destination country for smuggled cigarettes (13). He further details that in Greece, smuggled cigarettes are obtained by stealing from warehouses where they are stored, by importation from the Ukraine and Russia by ship, and by importation from Bulgaria by truck. Like elsewhere in the Balkans, Marlboro is a popular brand for smuggling.

It has a special appeal to the young who want to appear "westernized". According to research, contraband cigarettes represent 8 percent of total cigarette consumption in the country and the cigarette-smuggling business deprives the Greek state of millions in taxes (14).

Small gains have been made in curtailing smuggling. In 2010, European Union police broke up a Greek based gang that manufactured tax-free cigarettes and smuggled them into Germany. Of the 22 persons arrested, two were high ranking Greek police officers. In October 2011, two Chinese nationals were arrested by the police financial crimes squad. Contraband tobacco and cigarettes were found in 353 plastic bags hidden in crates filled with clothing. The investigation revealed that more such cargoes had been moved with the same process in the past. In this case, Greece's financial crimes police are collaborating with authorities in France, Britain, Europol and Interpol in an investigation of the case. The effect the current reduction of government employees in Greece will have on smuggling control is unknown.

Taxation

In accordance with a law common to EU member states a combination of ad valorem and specific excise tax are applied to cigarettes. The difference between ad valorem and specific taxes lies in how they are applied and, in the event of their change how they influence the final retail price of tobacco products. World Bank officials recommend using both types of excise to benefit from the combined effects. According to the Greek Reporting Instrument dated September 15, 2008, for EU produced tobacco products the excise tax is 57.5% of the retail price and the VAT is 15.97% of the retail price (15).

The three most popular cigarettes in Greece are Marlboro Red, G.R. and Assos Int. In most of EU countries, cigarette tax as a percentage of total tax revenue is small. The only exception is Greece. In 1999, cigarette tax accounted for about 9% of total government tax in Greece (16). This results in an economy that has a significant reliance on cigarette taxation as a source of revenue for the government.

Total tobacco tax as a proportion of retail price is 73.4% (17). The current (2011) price of Marlboro Red is 4 euro for a

20 cigarette pack and Asos Int. costs 3, 20 Euro for a 20 cigarette pack (18). To put this in perspective, the Greece Gross Domestic Product per capita on a purchasing power parity basis divided by population for 2010 was $29,600 (19). The price of cigarettes is even more significant in a country where unemployment is above the euro-zone average while per capita income is below. In 2011 prices, for the price of 20 Marlboro in Greece you could buy 3 liters of milk, 4 cans of beer, or 4 small loaves of bread in Greece.

Increased taxation on cigarettes is uniformly recommended as a method for decreasing consumption.

Conclusion

With some of the globe's highest smoking rates Greece can experience some of the greatest health benefits as well as increases in productivity from its tobacco control efforts. Treatments for tobacco dependence have the potential to reduce tobacco-related disease and many are highly cost-effective. It should be obvious that strict enforcement of nationwide anti-tobacco policies must be a priority on the national health agenda given the vulnerability of the Greek population to tobacco-related diseases. Despite the clear economic and health related gains of smoke free legislations, a notion that has been brought forward by restaurant and café owners is that smoke free legislation has an impact on the economy and will affect the revenue of the hospitality industry. Countries whose economies are under financial strain, such as those of Greece are susceptible to such pressure. Efforts should be made to stress that most well designed studies report that smoke free legislations has no effect on hospitality revenue (20).

Strategies for Greece are similar to those suggested for other Balkan countries and include; (1) cigarette tax increases, (2) publishing and disseminating research on the adverse health effects of tobacco, (3) complete restriction of smoking in the workplace and other public places, (4) control of smuggling and (5) widening access to a variety of smoke cessation therapies.

Greece is admittedly in a difficult position given its acute economic priorities. Recently, the government has shown very positive movement in the area of smoking and tobacco advertising bans. Although more work can be done, the country has made a strong start in moving in the direction of a forward thinking country with a concern for the health of the public.

References

1. Bloomberg L. P. (2011). Unemployment rate graph for GKUERATE Index (Greece Unemployment Rate Monthly) 01/31/04 to 8/31/11. Retrieved Nov. 30, 2011 from Bloomberg database

2. Greece Reporting Instrument to the European Union. September 15, 2008. Submitted by Mrs. Anastasia Pantazopoulou, Director of Public Health. Department of Public Health, Ministry of Health & Social Solidarity. Available at http://www.who.int/en/.

3. OECD Health Indicators, 2005. OECD publishing; Health at a Glance.

4. Linardakis, M, Sarri, K, Bervanaki, F, et al. Ten year evaluation of the initiation of a health education program in the schools of Crete. Paediatriki 2003; 66: 436-47 (in Greek).

5. Kokkevi A, Terzidou M., Politikou K, Stefanis, C. Substance use among high school students in Greece: outburst of illicit drug use in a society under change. Drug Alcohol Depend 2000; 58:181-8.

6. Varvadas, C, Bouloukaki, I, Linardakis, M, Tzilepi, P, Tzanakis, N & Kafatos, A. Smoke-free hospitals in Greece: Personnel perceptions, compliance and smoking habit. Short report. Tobacco Induced Diseases. March 2009.

7. Vardavas, C. & Kafatos, A. G. (2007) Bans on smoking in public places: policy enforcement needed. The Lancet; Jul 14-Jul 20, 2007; 370, 9582.

8. Tamvakas, I & Amos, A. (2010) Expand+'These things don't happen in Greece': a qualitative study of Greek young people's attitudes to smoking, secondhand smoke and the smoke free legislation. Health Educ. Res. 25 (6): 955-964.

9. Vardavas, C. Connolly, G. Karamanolis, K. Kafatos, A. (2009). Adolescents perceived effectiveness of the proposed European graphic tobacco warning labels. European Journal of Public Health, Vol. 19, No. 2, 212–217.

10. Labour Force Survey: April 2011 (PDF). Piraeus: Hellenic Statistical Authority. 19 July 2011. Available at: http://www.statistics.gr/portal/ page/portal/ESYE/BUCKET/A0101/PressReleases/A0101_SJO02_DT_ MM_04_2011_01_F_EN.pdf. Retrieved 19 July 2011.

11. McKay, J. & Erikson, M. 2002. The Tobacco Atlas, World Health Organization.

12. Conference Report CSD International Conference: Counteracting Cigarette Smuggling in the Balkans, Center for the Study of Democracy. Available at: http://www.csd.bg/artShow.php?id=15637.

13. Antonopoulos, G. A. (2006) Cigarette Smuggling: A Case Study of a Smuggling Network in Greece, European Journal of crime, Criminal Law and Criminal Justice. Vol. 14. 239-255.

14. Antonopoulos, G. A. (2007) 'The Greek connection(s): The social organization of the cigarette-smuggling business in Greece, European Journal of Criminology, 5(3), pp.263-288.

15. Greece Reporting Instrument to the European Union. September 15, 2008. Submitted by Mrs. Anastasia Pantazopoulou, Director of Public Health. Department of Public Health, Ministry of Health & Social Solidarity. Available at http://www.who.int/en/.

16. Regional report Europe (EU) Economics of Tobacco for the Europe (EU) Region. June 24, 2001.

17. Shafey O. et al. The Tobacco Atlas (2009). Third Edition. Table B. Available at :http://www.tobaccoatlas.org/downloads/TobaccoAtlas_sm.pdf retrieved 4 October 2011.

18. Personal correspondence October 1, 2011. Professor Felitsa Mullen, Thessaloniki, Greece.

19. CIA World Factbook. Available at: https://www.cia.gov/library/publications/the-world-factbook/geos/gr.html Retrieved 21 September 2011.

20. Scollo, M., Lal, A. Hyland, A. & Glantz, S. Review of the quality of studies on the economic effects of smoke-free policies on the hospitality industry. Tobacco Control 2003;12:13-20.

Conclusion

The World Health Organization created and led the Framework Convention on Tobacco Control. Adopted in 2003, with the participation of 300 organizations worldwide, the framework has initiated activities to reduce the nearly 5 million deaths attributable to tobacco use every year and has worked with governments to raise their understanding of relevant scientific research (1). No one would argue that measures to reduce smoking are one of the most effective public health initiatives that any country can institute. The success of the United States, Canada, and Western Europe in reducing tobacco consumption has been one of the public health achievements of this century. This is not the case in the Balkans. The officials (government leaders) of four of the countries under review in this book could be doing more to fight the health effects of tobacco. This is a large challenge in countries that to a greater or lesser degree are struggling to move toward a market economy while combating economic pressures, unemployment, corruption, and crime. These Balkan nations are all considered to be low or middle-income countries. While the suggested measures seem rather simplistic on the surface, implementation in the evolving economies of Croatia, Romania, Bulgaria, and Greece can admittedly be complicated efforts.

The four countries included in this book have some similarities but also differ significantly in their smoking prevalence, in their economic status and in their tobacco control programs. What is consistent is that governments aim to reduce tobacco consumption now and in the future. What also is consistent is that these countries want to be part of the EU and must comply with specific smoking legislation in order to do so. It is a given that people have an inherent right to receive information about the direct and indirect harms of tobacco use (2) and countries have an obligation to provide it. A common thread that emerges is the tension between the public health efforts to reduce tobacco consumption and the economic constraints of fledgling market driven capitalistic societies (Croatia, Bulgaria, and Romania) or of economically challenged economies (Greece).

Monitoring and Data Collection

Strong international monitoring of the tobacco epidemic is basic to knowing where we stand. Central to this effort is the effective and ongoing systematic collection of valid and reliable data that could be compared among nations. Data collection should include not only accurate data on smoking prevalence but information on imports, exports, sales, and the consumption of both legally and illegally purchased cigarettes. This data then needs to be disseminated to those who need to know in a timely manner. In order to assess and evaluate the progress with decreasing smoking in the European Union this information is primordial. This is a matter of concern since the European Commission (EC) has only measured by sampling the percentage of people smoking in member states on four occasions (2002, 2005, 2006 and 2008). This information should be collected yearly and on a uniform basis. The WHO Framework Convention on Tobacco Control collects data on tobacco statistics by country but the reporting periods for each country are not standardized.

In a study that examined survey methods used from country to country it was determined that various survey factors such as question construction, sample size, and age range varied among countries (3). For example, smoking of oral tobacco is banned by law in Romania, yet the government maintains no statistics on its use. Although, Romania is a country that is composed of distinct ethnic communities (the Roma for example) it does not maintain any current statistics on prevalence by ethnicity. Further, national and European Commission survey estimates are highly discrepant.

Monitoring national smoking statistics on a consistent and regular basis is essential to measuring incidence, prevalence and the effect of various public health efforts. Comparisons of prevalence figures by age group have been hard to make on account of the variety of age groups for which EU members provide data. This data needs to be standardized and distributed to public health officials, politicians, the general citizenry and to those who implement smoking control efforts. Only with good data and monitoring will we know if public health efforts are working and how they should be tailored to different regions. It is a public health failure to not consider the problems that arise from lack of information. In the long run, the social benefit of acquiring information may outweigh the cost of acquisition.

Advertising Ban

Tobacco is one of the most dangerous consumer products advertised today. There is no safe or moderate level of smoking. The freedom to advertise can and should be restricted for health reasons. One of the major public health targets is to implement a complete advertising ban on all tobacco products. None of the countries has managed that. While some have banned all forms of direct advertising, none have banned both indirect and direct advertising. Advertising at point of sale (gas stations, retail outlets, kiosks..,) is permitted in all countries. Some countries, like Bulgaria, have delayed public smoking bans in the belief that the hospitality industry will be affected adversely. No credible evidence exists to support this supposition. In fact, credible scientific studies indicate that no negative economic impacts of these policies occurred.

Taxation

The European Union Council of Ministers, the principal decision-making body, has adopted a directive updating EU rules on the structure and rates of excise duties on cigarettes and other tobacco products(4). The directive is intended to ensure a higher level of public health protection by raising minimum excise duties on cigarettes. The general level of taxation for cigarettes is high in EU countries. Tobacco taxation in Romania, Bulgaria, and Greece have not yet achieved, or only recently achieved, the current monetary minimum excise rates set by the EU Council of Ministers. A 2005 report of the structure of taxation of tobacco products in Europe indicated that total taxes often exceed 75% of the price of cigarettes when value-added tax (VAT) is included. The Balkan countries in this review all have total tax structures of less than 75% (5). It is a myth that only western (AKA wealthy) countries can have tobacco control regulations that raise taxes and that poor countries cannot afford them. The reality is actually the opposite. The true cost of tobacco addiction has been proven irrefutably to be a high societal cost and increase taxation is an appropriate treatment of choice. It is argued that increase taxation will lead to unemployment in the agricultural and retail sector. This concern has been fueled by the tobacco industry. Jobs lost in retailing tobacco will most probably be replaced by jobs selling other products that people purchase with the money previously spent on cigarettes. In perspective, tobacco cultivation is a small part of most of the economies in the Balkans. Farmers could shift to alternative crops if current tobacco prices did not persist. Generally, tobacco is grown in sunny locations in well drained soil. This type of landage can accommodate a variety of crops although there does not seem to be any government programs toward successful diversification towards economically sustainable alternatives to tobacco growing. As these countries become more westernized their economies will naturally shift more toward service economies. This is already happening in the Balkans and will naturally result in less reliance on agricultural products such as tobacco.

These four countries tend to be low and medium income countries. In this situation, increasing the cost of cigarettes through increased taxation can lead to decreased consumption. The results of one study indicate that a 10% increase in cigarette prices would reduce consumption by 8% in low and middle-income countries (6). With an increase in the cigarette tax, the resultant decline in consumption will also lead to a decline in health care costs as former smokers and their children require less medical care. It will also result in decrease government revenues. Although more progress can be made, it is important to note the progress of Bulgaria and Romania as they are listed as one of the highest achieving countries in 2010 for increasing tobacco prices through higher taxes. This is the case despite tobacco companies utilizing a range of self serving strategies to influence tobacco taxation to their benefit.

Some countries have earmarked tobacco taxes for health endeavors. Other countries have added a given percentage to the excise tax in order to collect revenue for special purposes, including health, while others earmark a given share of collected tobacco taxes. Only eleven countries out of 117 that report tobacco control efforts to the World Health Organization currently subscribe to this form of taxation (7). Bulgaria, to its credit is one of these countries. In general, social media or social networking sites such as Facebook, Linked-in, Svejo.net and blogs are one of the least used media for anti-tobacco messages in Eastern Europe. This is a prevalent communications method among Generation Y or Millenial cohorts who are an age group that is particularly vulnerable to starting to smoke. Use of these platforms is common among youth in Bulgaria, Croatia, Romania, and Greece. Earmarking tobacco taxes toward these media forms could be an especially potent form of communicating anti-tobacco messages to a young age group.

Smuggling

Greece, Bulgaria, Romania and Croatia are particularly vulnerable to smuggling given their geography. The Balkan Peninsula of southeastern Europe is surrounded by water on three sides: the Adriatic Sea to the west, the Mediterranean Sea to the south and the Black Sea to the east. Greece and Croatia have many large and small islands. Waterways are often more difficult to control from the viewpoint of smuggling than land borders. Croatia, Romania, Bulgaria, and Greece all have direct sea access that lends itself to all varieties of smuggling activities. Romania is vulnerable as it borders former USSR countries where corruption and smuggling proliferates.

Smuggled goods include alcohol, petrol, diamonds, weapons, antiques, drugs, and cigarettes. Of all types of smuggled goods, cigarettes are the most widely smuggled legal consumer product. It is estimated that between 6% and 8.5% of global cigarette consumption is smuggled (8). Cigarette smuggling is a very big business in Croatia, Bulgaria, Romania, and Greece. Smuggling causes major harm as it promotes smoking by lowering cigarette prices. Where variations in cigarette tax exist between countries, corruption occurs, and contraband sales are tolerated, cigarette smuggling is a problem. Smuggled cigarettes can affect disproportionate harm to the younger smokers by undermining efforts to limit underage access to tobacco products. While there is no guarantee that retailers will verify that youth meet the legal age for purchasing cigarettes, it is much less likely that vendors of smuggled cigarettes will comply with national policies in this regard. Despite its broad impact on health and taxes, tobacco smuggling receives strikingly little serious attention from governmental authorities.

Even if tobacco smugglers are convicted, lenient sentences are the norm. Cigarette smuggling is not considered a serious crime by people in the Balkans. On a more global scale, the people involved in illicit cigarette trade are targeted by organized crime and then involved in other criminal activities such as drugs and prostitution, thereby increasing the social impact of such activities.

Even when anti-smuggling legislation is strengthened tobacco problems transcend boundaries and even if a country is committed they cannot solve them nationally. Resolution will require international collaboration. Romania and Bulgaria have not been allowed to join the Schengen agreement because of their lack of adequate control of their borders. Romania, Greece, Croatia, and Bulgaria have all reported an increase in the seizure of illicit tobacco products between the most recent reporting period and the previous reporting period. Over recent years, the trend is increasing of the percentage of smuggled tobacco products in relation to the national tobacco market.

Admittedly there is very little empirical research on the effectiveness of different anti-smuggling measures. Some have suggested that the tobacco companies be held responsible for ensuring that cigarettes arrive legally at their point of sale in the marketplace and be liable if the product ends up smuggled. Others suggest introducing measures such as licensing all participants in the tobacco business. State-of-the-art tracking and tracing system for all manufactured tobacco products would allow effective monitoring of a product's distribution chain and any diversions, while facilitating the identification of illicit products. This system would more than pay for itself in increased tax revenues. At minimum, the penalties for smuggling tobacco products should be increased in all countries.

Economic theory suggests that TDR, Bulgartabac, and other tobacco companies benefit from smuggling and they are aware of the extent of smuggling. One tobacco company performed a market research study in one of the capital cities to determine the extent of smuggling. They hired a market research firm to collect all the discarded tobacco packs in public garbage bins for a given period. The discarded packs were sorted into those that had the appropriate tax stamp and those that did not. In this way, they were able to get an approximation of the percentage of smuggled cigarettes in that city. It should be noted that the tobacco industry in general benefits from smuggling, as it lowers the price paid in average by the consumer, increasing consumption and thus, tobacco sales. Tobacco company executives do not care if taxes are paid as long as market share increases. Smuggled cigarettes involve imported brands that are not available in the country. These brands are viewed as "prestige' brands and are sought by young adults who are a highly vulnerable cohort of smokers. Despite rhetoric to the contrary, involving the tobacco companies in the solution will be challenging

Smuggling is not only stimulated by tax increases and price differentials but it is consonant with general corruption. Bulgaria, Romania, Greece and to a lesser extent Croatia are all known to have higher indexes of corruption than other countries in Western Europe. Transparency International is a global network including more than 90 locally established national chapters. The goal of this organization is to fight corruption in the national arena. Transparency International publishes a 2010 Corruption Perceptions Index (CPI). The 2010 CPI measures the degree to which public sector corruption is perceived to exist in 178 countries around the world. It scores countries on a scale from 10 (very clean) to 0 (highly corrupt). All four of these countries score less than 5 on the CPI. Croatia scores 4.1, Romania scores 3.7, Bulgaria scores 3.6 and Greece scores 3.5. By comparison, Germany scores 7.9, France 6.8, and Spain scores 6.1 (9). These results indicate a serious corruption problem. Corruption and smuggling are inextricably linked. One cannot be battled without also targeting the other. A number of policy options have been suggested to control smuggling including revised labeling, tracking and licensing systems, chain of custody markings, more enforcement and higher penalties. Finally, smuggling is often viewed by the general populace as a "victimless crime". Social

marketing campaigns and other efforts to raise consumer awareness could be used by the health department to raise consciousness concerning the problems associated with smuggling.

Governmental Legislation

National legislation regarding smoking differs widely across EU
Member States. For example, most Member States have regulations
banning or restricting smoking in major public places, such as
health care, educational and government facilities, theatres,
cinemas, and public transport (10). Ireland, Italy, Malta, Sweden
and parts of the United Kingdom (Wales and Scotland) have
been cited as having excellent examples of effective measures
to protect their citizens from the harmful effects of passive
smoking.   Although Croatia, Bulgaria, Greece and Romania have
laws making certain environments smoke free, the laws are not
as aggressive in the five countries just cited. They would do well
to adopt anti-cigarette smoking laws similar to those in effect in
Ireland, Italy, Malta, Sweden and the United Kingdom. Overall,
cultural facilities in these four countries seem to be the best
protected from exposure to tobacco smoke. At the other end of
the scale are bars and nightclubs. In the Balkans, but especially
in Bulgaria, smoking in bars and nightclubs is the norm rather
than the exception. In general, workers are better protected in
health-care facilities and educational facilities than in private
workplaces. Croatia, Bulgaria, Romania, and Greece have laws
making certain environments smoke-free although they are less
stringent in their legislation than other countries.

Compliance with these laws is certainly an issue particularly
in the Balkans where the culture is one of acceptance of smoking behavior. The role of non-smokers has not been completely
investigated in the Balkans. For example, 57% of Croatian people
reported that they would never ask a smoker to stop smoking
because it bothered them (11). The Balkan countries tend to have

a citizenry that are reluctant to speak up and assert their rights as non smokers. Policymakers should evaluate how non-smokers could actively support smoke-free laws through reporting of violations. Social marketing campaigns could also be used to inform them of their rights and encourage them to speak up.

It is important to pause and provide a sense of perspective. As compared to parts of Western Europe, the countries in the Balkans are less accustomed to government intervention in the choices of consumers. It is generally acknowledged that adults should be allowed to make their own informed choices (12). Adults are legally entitled to smoke cigarettes. Public opinion and policymaking in the Balkans has tended to emphasize freedom of choice to smoke. Clearly individuals of age have a right to smoke if it does not impinge on the rights of others. There are certain decisions that should not be left up to children and adolescents. The right to begin smoking is one of them. In general, youth restrictions are difficult to enforce given that young teenagers often obtain cigarettes from their older peers. In low-income countries such as the Balkan countries of Romania, Bulgaria, and Croatia, the necessary systems, infrastructure, and resources for implementing such restrictions and enforcing them are much less widely available than in the high-income countries. It is wise then to develop health information programs for specific subgroups of the population. Children, adolescents and pregnant women are groups that are at high risk and need this particular focus. As a modern society, however, it is imperative that all citizens fully comprehend the individual and collective hazards of smoking and be provided with public assistance to quit if desired.

Clean Indoor Air

The development of any public policy about tobacco control would be incomplete without considering the importance of clean indoor air. Numerous studies have shown that clean indoor air policies result in reduction in smoking consumption and there is a clear trend towards smoke-free environments throughout the EU. The risk of secondhand (environmental) tobacco smoke (ETS) is well documented in the literature. Although the level of individual risk is lower than active smoking, adverse health outcomes from ETS are clear. The Institute of Medicine report (2007) notes that smoking restrictions serve three purposes: (1) they protect nonsmoker from the health effects and the noxious odors of secondhand smoke; (2) they help smokers quit, cut down on their smoking, and avoid relapses; and (3) they reinforce a non smoking norm (13). The main places for chronic and intensive ETS exposure are the home and the workplace (14). The impact of a smoke-free initiative in the workplace has the benefit of not only protecting people from the harm of ETS but also contributes to the reduction of tobacco consumption in the whole population. All of the countries have some type of ban of smoking in the workplace. A sample of convenience of large companies (over 500 employees) in Zagreb Croatia in 2008 shows that they have made good progress in formally adopting the law regarding smoking in the workplace at least on paper (15). Research is needed to assess actual in situ compliance.

Fines for ignoring the rules regulating smoking in the workplace are minimal. In Croatia, for example, violators of the law can be fined less than 20 euros. One of the reasons the rules regulating smoking tend to be ignored is ineffective fines assessed to violators. Unfortunately, there are no available statistics on the number of fines collected. Declaring the work environment smoke-free without proper control mechanisms that will actually deal with violators leads to implementation of the law on paper and not in practice. Enforcement of all smoke-free legislation in the Balkans should not be insulated from democratic accountability.

Pictorial Warnings

The European Commission requires tobacco products sold in the European Union to display standardized text health warnings.

Graphic pictures on cigarette packs of the negative effects of smoking are termed pictorial warnings and they are a valid social marketing tool for communicating the health risks of tobacco use. Pictorial warnings are an especially promising public health strategy because of their low cost to government regulators and their wide reach among smokers. These warnings convey health information, decrease the attractiveness of cigarettes and counter the alluring images used by tobacco companies to market cigarettes.

The first year that pictorial markings appeared on cigarettes was 2001 and Belgium was the first country to require pictures or images on cigarette packs. Research has shown that larger warnings with pictures are significantly more effective than smaller, text-only messages (16). In 2011, the US Food and Drug Administration (FDA) released nine new warning labels that depict in graphic detail the negative health effects of tobacco use. The labels were projected to take up the top half both front and back of a pack of cigarettes. This requirement, which is one of the most significant changes in US cigarette packs in 25 years, was to be effective in 2012. In addition to graphic warnings, each pack would contain a national quit smoking hot line number. Claiming that the regulation violates their constitutional rights, tobacco giant RJ Reynolds and others have filed suit to block the regulation. In 2011, a federal judge blocked a U.S. rule requiring tobacco companies to display graphic images on cigarette packs. Tobacco manufacturers argued that the graphic warnings force them to 'engage in anti-smoking advocacy" on the governments behalf and violate their right of free speech. The case will most probably reach the US Supreme Court. The efficacy of pictorial warnings may explain why tobacco companies have strenuously opposed comprehensive cigarette warnings.

Canada introduced pictorial warnings and smoking rates have declined from approximately 26% to about 20%. (17). With respect to pictorial warnings on cigarette packs, Romania is one of the few European countries to require them. Greece, Bulgaria, and

Croatia have no such requirement. A study of Greek adolescents found that proposed EU pictorial warnings were more effective at informing about the health effects of smoking and preventing initiation than the text only warnings (18). Interestingly, the majority (75%) of Europeans are in favor of putting picture health warnings on all packages of tobacco products (19). Arguments can be presented to increase the size of the pictorial warnings to 80% of the pack, to regularly rotate warning messages to prevent the graphic images from becoming "normalized", and to include information on the packaging about a 'quit line' to help stop smoking. A smoker who consumes a pack of cigarettes per day would have 7300 potential opportunities per year to view an anti-smoking image. Another important strategy would be to target potential warnings to specific high risk groups such as youth. Effectively providing youth with warnings requires approaches different among cultures and among age groups. Relatively straightforward and inexpensive market research could determine which warnings are more likely to change behavior among youth groups in South Eastern Europe and other market segments.

Conclusion

The operating assumptions of tobacco control policies in the Balkans are changing. Policy making on tobacco control efforts was shaped by economic conditions, state controlled tobacco companies, consumer freedom of choice, and cultural norms. As Croatia, Bulgaria, Romania, and Greece have become more westernized and public understanding of the harms of smoking has deepened, policymaking has moved in the direction of reducing tobacco consumption. For these countries, progress has been slow, has occurred in fits and starts, and still has a long way to go.

In every society, there are challenges facing citizens, governmental agencies, and the political leadership. Tobacco use is one of those high priority challenges for the Balkans. Tobacco use has exacted a tragic toll on the population of the world in general and the countries of Croatia, Bulgaria, Romania, and Greece in particular. The issues of tobacco control in the Balkans defy simple summarization. There is no question that in general public resources are limited and that this is especially true in the Balkans where the countries lag economically behind much of the developed Western Europe. It is an economic reality that public health spending must compete with other valid causes such as an underdeveloped infrastructure which is common to Croatia, Romania, Greece and especially Bulgaria. It has been well documented that a sound infrastructure is one of the important prerequisites for a developed economy. It is not said lightly then that the efforts of the public health sector to garner a share of government revenue for anti-smoking efforts is a herculean task. Lack of financial transparency in these countries contributes to the magnitude of this effort. It would be unrealistic to envision that these countries would reduce their tobacco consumption to an arbitrarily chosen low percentage of smoking prevalence. That challenge has little practical significance in the Balkans. The Institute of Medicine report (2007) suggests that for the next decade or two, the aim must be to reduce initiation and increase cessation as much as possible without stimulating a substantial black market and its associated costs (20). Efforts in the Balkans to reduce cigarette consumption will have long term effects on the financial stability of the region through decreasing the untoward health effects and lost productivity from smoking. This is a major challenge for public health professionals and government leaders alike.

References

1.   Bloom, David E., (2007) Governing Global Health. Finance and Development Vol. 44. No. 4. International Monetary Fund.

2. Chapman S et al. Ensuring smokers are adequately informed: reflections on consumer rights, manufacturer responsibilities, and policy implications. Tobacco Control, 2005, 14(Suppl.2): ii8-ii13.

3. Bogdanovica, I., Godfrey, F., & Britton, J. (2011) Smoking Prevalence in the European Union: a comparison of national and transnational prevalence survey methods and results. Tobacco Control 20 (1).

4. EU to increase cigarette and tobacco excises. 2/16/2010. The Sophia Echo (staff).Available from http://www.sofiaecho.com/2010/02/16/859049_eu-to-increase-cigarette-and-tobacco-excises?&lang=en_us&output=json&session-id=907f51b8ee737ad747e57b499928c069.

5. The European Tobacco Control Report. World Health Organization. Regional Office for Europe; 2007 [cited 2010 Dec. 9]. Available from http://www.euro.who.int/__data/assets/pdf_file/0005/68117/E89842.pdf.

6. Ranson K, Jha P, Chaloupka F, Nguyen S. The effectiveness and cost-effectiveness of price increases and other tobacco control policies. In: Jha P, Chaloupka F, eds. Tobacco Control in Developing Countries. Oxford, England: Oxford University Press; 2000.

7. WHO Framework Convention on Tobacco Control (2009) Summary Report on global progress in implementation of the WHO Framework Convention on Tobacco Control. Accessed at: http://www.wpro.who.int/nr/rdonlyres/d7077780-b94f-4cc3-ac4a-d223c69191e9/0/fctc-2009summary_report.pdf.

8. Jha, Prabhat & Chaloupka, F. Ed. Tobacco Control in Developing Countries. Oxford University Press; 2000.

9. Corruption Perceptions Index 2010. Transparency International. Available at: http://www.transparency.org/policy_research/surveys_indices/cpi/2010/results.

10. Health and Consumer Protection Directorate General, European Commission Green Paper Towards a Europe Free from Tobacco Smoke: Policy Options at the EU Level: January 2007.

11. Attitudes of Europeans Towards Tobacco: Special Eurobarometer 239 [monograph on the internet]. Brussels: European Commission; 2006 [cited 2008 May 20]. Available fromURL http://www.ec.europa.cu/ health/ph_information/documents/ cbs_293_en.pdf.

12. Tobacco Control in Developing Countries Edited by Prabhat Jha and Frank J. Chaloupka. 512 pp., illustrated. New York, Oxford University Press, 2000.

13. Bonnie RJ, Stratton K, Wallace RB, editors. Ending the Tobacco Problem. Washington (DC): Institute of Medicine of the National Academies; 2007.

14. Philips K, Howard D, Brown D, et al. Assessment of Personal Exposure to Environmental Tobacco Smoke in British Non Smokers. Environnemental International. 1994; 20: 693-712.

15. Loubeau, P. Unpublished study. (2008) Compliance with No-Smoking Regulation in Zagreb Companies. 2008.

16. Hammond, D. Health warning messages on tobacco products: a review. Tobacco Control. 2011; 20:327-337.

17. Felderbaum, M. FDA issues graphic cigarette labels. Spartanburg Herald Journal. June 21, 2011.

18. Vardavas, CI et al, Adolescents perceived effectiveness of the proposed European graphic tobacco warning labels, European Journal of Public Health, 19(2):212-7, 2009.

19. Tobacco Special Eurobarometer 332/Wave 72.3- TNS Opinion & Social. May 2010.

20. Institute of Medicine of the National Academies (2007) Ending the Tobacco Problem: A Blueprint for the Nation. The National Academies Press. Washington, D.C.

About the Author

Patricia Loubeau has worked and travelled extensively in Eastern Europe. She is currently Professor of Marketing and International Business at Iona College, New Rochelle, NY. She received her BS and MPH in Health Care Management from the University of Pittsburgh. She holds a doctorate in Health Policy and Management from Columbia University. In 2008, she served as a Fulbright Fellow at the Zagreb School of Economics and Management in Zagreb Croatia. In 2011 she spent a year as a Visiting Professor in the Department of Business Administration at the American University of Bulgaria in Blagoevgrad, Bulgaria. She has published extensively in the area of marketing, public health issues, and health economics.

Made in the USA
San Bernardino, CA
21 August 2013